JN122195

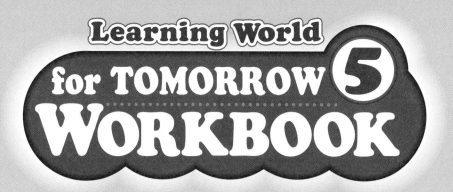

CONTENTS

🌐 Unit 1    2～7

🌐 Unit 2    8～13

🌐 Unit 3    14～19

🌐 Unit 4    20～25

🌐 Unit 5    26～31

🌐 Unit 6    32～37

🌐 Unit 7    38～43

🌐 Unit 8    44～49

🌐 Unit 9    50～55

🌐 Unit 10   56～61

Let's try. 1    63

Let's try. 2    64

Let's try. 3    65

Let's try. 4    66

Let's try. 5    68    CD 31

Listening Test 1, 2    70    CD 7～18

Listening Test 3, 4    71    CD 19～30

**Let's try.** のページは英検3級レベルの問題です。

"**Let's try.**" and "**Listening Test**" pages are designed for EIKEN Test Grade 3 questions.

※答えおよび音声スクリプトは本ワークブックの最終ページに付いています。 切り取ってお使いいただけます。

■ 別冊フルカラー20ページ： **Cambridge English: Movers (YLE Movers)**
ヤングラーナーズ英語検定(YLE)ムーバーズ

練習問題

| ■ Listening | 別冊 pp. 4-9 | |
| --- | --- | --- |
| Part 1 | 別冊 p. 4 | CD 1 |
| Part 2 | 別冊 p. 5 | CD 2 |
| Part 3 | 別冊 p. 6 | CD 3 |
| Part 4 | 別冊 p. 7 | CD 4 |
| Part 5 | 別冊 p. 9 | CD 5 |
| ■ Reading and Writing | 別冊 pp. 10-23 | |

本ワークブックから1枚ずつゆっくりと引っ張れば外すことも可能です。

※答えおよび音声スクリプトは TOMORROW 指導書に記載しています。

# Unit 1 ①

## 1 📖 Words / Phrases

1. introduce ( ) _____
2. famous ( ) _____
3. blood ( ) _____
4. instrument ( ) _____
5. organized ( ) _____
6. intelligent ( ) _____
7. thunderstorm ( ) _____
8. height ( ) _____
9. gardening ( ) _____
10. ironing ( ) _____
11. family name ( ) _____
12. good listener ( ) _____
13. of course ( ) _____
14. being alone ( ) _____
15. a member of ( ) _____
16. being on my own ( ) _____

## 2 Read Daichi's speech on p.4 of the textbook and answer the questions.

1. What is his name? _____
2. Does he have a brother? _____
3. How old is he? _____
4. Can he run fast? _____
5. Is he a member of the baseball team? _____
6. What subject does he like? _____
7. Does his father teach math? _____
8. Is his mother good at singing? _____

**3** **Answer the following questions.**

**1** Are you a high school student?

_____

_____

**2** Do you like vegetables?

_____

_____

**3** Does your mother speak English?

_____

_____

**4** Can you cook dinner for your family?

_____

_____

**5** Is your homeroom teacher strict?

_____

_____

**6** How do you usually come to school?

_____

_____

**7** Can you play any musical instruments?

_____

_____

**8** Does your teacher have a pet?

_____

_____

**9** Is your teacher good at singing?

_____

_____

**10** Is it raining now?

_____

_____

**11** Was it raining last night?

_____

_____

**12** Did you go to school yesterday?

_____

_____

**13** Did you stay up late last night?

_____

_____

**14** Are you going to study English tonight?

_____

_____

## 1 📖 Words/Phrases

| | | | | |
|---|---|---|---|---|
| ① | spin ( ) _____ | | ⑨ | face ( ) _____ |
| ② | go around ( ) _____ | | ⑩ | light ( ) _____ |
| ③ | morning ( ) _____ | | ⑪ | heat ( ) _____ |
| ④ | afternoon ( ) _____ | | ⑫ | the other ( ) _____ |
| ⑤ | evening ( ) _____ | | ⑬ | axis ( ) _____ |
| ⑥ | night ( ) _____ | | ⑭ | season ( ) _____ |
| ⑦ | day ( ) _____ | | ⑮ | identify ( ) _____ |
| ⑧ | cause ( ) _____ | | ⑯ | daytime ( ) _____ |

## 2 Rewrite the sentences using the present continuous tense. 現在進行形にしましょう。
If the sentence cannot be written in the present continuous, write it as is. 進行形にする必要のないものはそのまま書きましょう。

① You study English. ▷ _____

② Tom runs in the park. ▷ _____

③ You wash your father's car. ▷ _____

④ JJ and I have lunch together. ▷ _____

⑤ She does her homework. ▷ _____

⑥ We read the newspaper. ▷ _____

⑦ You have a sister. ▷ _____

⑧ She knows Kevin very well. ▷ _____

**3 Rewrite the previous sentences as questions, and then answer them with "Yes" or "No".**
2 で書いた英文を疑問文にし、Yes, No で答えましょう。

**1** Q Are you

Yes,                                              No,

**2** Q

Yes,                                              No,

**3** Q

Yes,                                              No,

**4** Q

Yes,                                              No,

**5** Q

Yes,                                              No,

**6** Q

Yes,                                              No,

**7** Q

Yes,                                              No,

**8** Q

Yes,                                              No,

**4 What causes night and day? :** After reading the passage on p.7 of the textbook, write about it.
テキストp.7の英文を読んで、なぜ昼と夜があるのかを書きましょう。

## 1 📖 Words / Phrases

1 gentleman ( ) _____

2 bank ( ) _____

3 sunflower ( ) _____

4 population ( ) _____

5 smart ( ) _____

6 sincere ( ) _____

7 honest ( ) _____

8 adventurous ( ) _____

9 athletic ( ) _____

10 tough ( ) _____

11 optimistic ( ) _____

12 energetic ( ) _____

13 diligent ( ) _____

14 ambitious ( ) _____

15 humorous ( ) _____

16 unique ( ) _____

## 2 〜ですか？ Make the sentences into questions.

1 There are many stars in the sky. ▶ Are there _____

2 There is a red cap on the desk. ▶ _____

3 There are four seasons in a year in Japan.
▶ _____

## 3 〜でない Rewrite the sentences using not.

1 There is a good coffee shop near my house.
▶ There is not _____

2 There are four seasons in a year in Hawaii.
▶ _____

3 There are many cars in the parking lot.
▶ _____

## 4 Complete the sentences to match the Japanese.

① テーブルの上にクッキーが数枚あります。ご自由にどうぞ。

There ＿＿＿＿＿＿＿＿ ＿＿＿＿＿＿＿＿ cookies ＿＿＿＿＿ the table.  Help yourself.

② この近くに書店はありますか？

Is ＿＿＿＿＿＿＿ a bookstore near ＿＿＿＿＿＿？

③ 冷蔵庫に牛乳が全くありません。

There ＿＿＿＿＿＿＿＿ any milk in the fridge.

④ あなたのクラスには何人生徒がいますか？

＿＿＿＿＿＿＿ ＿＿＿＿＿＿＿＿ students ＿＿＿＿＿ ＿＿＿＿＿ in your class?

⑤ 床には足跡がたくさん残っていました。

There ＿＿＿＿＿＿＿ a lot of footprints left ＿＿＿＿＿＿＿ the floor.

⑥ 私たちの間には誤解がたくさんあります。

There ＿＿＿＿＿＿＿ a lot of misunderstandings ＿＿＿＿＿＿＿ you and me.

## 5 Write your own answers.

**1** Is there a big library in your town?

**2** Is there an air conditioner in your classroom?

**3** How many days are there in a year?

**4** Do you think you are ambitious?

**5** Do you think you are optimistic?

**6** Do you think you are friendly?

**7** Do you think you are humorous?

## 1 📖 Words / Phrases

① Nice to see you again. ( )  _____

② Have a seat. ( )  _____

③ Make yourself at home. ( )  _____

④ Have some cookies. ( )  _____

⑤ Help yourself. ( )  _____

⑥ It was fun. ( )  _____

⑦ Hope to see you again. ( )  _____

⑧ Say hello to your family. ( )  _____

⑨ Keep in touch. ( )  _____

⑩ E-mail me. ( )  _____

## 2 Complete the sentences to match the Japanese.

① I am very happy to _____ _____ .  あなたにお会いできてとてもうれしいです。

② I am _____ _____ hear the news.  その知らせを聞いて驚きました。

③ I am happy _____ _____ _____ .  ここにいることができて嬉しいです。

④ She looks sad _____ _____ about the accident.  彼女は事故について聞いて悲しそうです。

⑤ He will be delighted _____ _____ this letter.  彼はこの手紙を読んで喜ぶでしょう。

⑥ I was relieved _____ _____ her at the gate.  搭乗口に彼女を見つけてほっとしました。

**3** **Various Greetings:** Draw a line to connect the English and Japanese sentences.

ダイアログと日本語を結んで覚えましょう。

A: Long time no see.
B: I'm so glad to see you.

A: How've you been?
B: Just fine.

A: Thank you.
B: It's my pleasure.

A: Have a happy new year.
B: Thank you. You too.

A: It was nice seeing you, again.
B: It was nice seeing you, too.

A: Is this seat taken?
B: No, it's empty.

A: Hello. This is Ken.
B: Hi, Ken. Hold on a second.
　 I'll get Cindy.

A: よいお年を。
B: ありがとう。あなたもね。

［電話で］A: もしもし。ケンです。
　　　　 B: やあケン。ちょっと待って。
　　　　　　シンディを呼ぶから。

A: 久しぶり。
B: 会えてうれしいです。

(席をゆびさして)
A: どなたかいらっしゃいます？
B: いいえ空いています。

A: どうしてたの？
B: 元気だったよ。

A: またあなたに会えてよかった。
B: 私もあなたに会えてよかった。

A: ありがとう。
B: どういたしまして。

**4** **Introduce someone:** Complete the sentences to match the Japanese.

Dr. Watson, this is my ＿＿＿＿＿＿ Emily.  She is a ＿＿＿＿＿＿ at Washington Hospital.

Emily, ＿＿＿＿＿＿ is Dr. Watson.  She is my ＿＿＿＿＿＿ teacher at Washington University.

ワトソン博士、こちらは私の友人のエミリーさんです。彼女はワシントン病院の医者です。

エミリー、こちらはワトソン博士です。彼女はワシントン大学の科学の先生です。

# 1 📖 Words／Phrases

1 dolphin ( )
2 taste ( )
3 remember ( )
4 crow ( )
5 for years ( )
6 more than ( )
7 sea horse ( )
8 give birth ( )

9 weigh ( )
10 dentist ( )
11 question ( )
12 blood type ( )
13 answer ( )
14 often ( )
15 only ( )
16 fact ( )

# 2 Make the sentences into questions.

1 Only male lions hunt.

2 Squids have ten legs.

3 Giraffes have very short tongues.

4 The sweat of hippos is blue.

5 Tigers get angry when you step on their tails.

6 Male mosquitoes bite and sip the blood of humans.

7 The tails of pandas are black.

**3 Answer the previous questions and write the correct answers if the answer is "no".**

2 で書いた質問文に対して Yes か No で答えましょう。No の場合は正しい情報を調べて英語にしましょう。

**1**

**2**

**3**

**4**

**5**

**6**

**7**

**4 Write your own answers.**

1 How many hearts do you have?

2 How many teeth do human adults have?

3 Do you have relatives in Tokyo?

4 Do you wake up without an alarm clock?

## 1 📖 Words/Phrases

| | | | | |
|---|---|---|---|---|
| ① | caterpillar ( ) | | ⑨ | arm ( ) |
| ② | leaf ( ) | | ⑩ | astronaut ( ) |
| ③ | butterfly ( ) | | ⑪ | space ( ) |
| ④ | mud ( ) | | ⑫ | one day ( ) |
| ⑤ | tadpole ( ) | | ⑬ | difference ( ) |
| ⑥ | pond ( ) | | ⑭ | between ( ) |
| ⑦ | frog ( ) | | ⑮ | story ( ) |
| ⑧ | land ( ) | | ⑯ | draw ( ) |

## 2 Rewrite the sentences using the past tense and will be. 次の文を過去形と未来形にしましょう。

① I am very busy today.
  ▷ I was very busy _____ yesterday.
  ▷ I will be very busy _____ tomorrow.

② Yumi and I are good friends.
  ▷ _____ in elementary school.
  ▷ _____ in the future.

③ My father is sick in bed today.
  ▷ _____ last week.
  ▷ _____ tomorrow.

④ Where are you?
  ▷ _____ last night?
  ▷ _____ tomorrow afternoon?

**❸**

**3** **Complete the sentences to match the Japanese.**

① **Q** あなたたちは、きのうの放課後どこにいたのですか？　　**A** 私たちは図書室にいました。

**Q** Where _____ you after school yesterday?　**A** We _____ at the _____ .

② **Q** 何をしていたのですか？　　　　　　　　　　　**A** 部屋のそうじをしていました。

**Q** _____ _____ you _____ ?　**A** We _____ cleaning the room.

③ **Q** その時、久美はきみたちと一緒でしたか？　　　**A** 一緒ではなかったです。

**Q** _____ Kumi _____ you at that time?　**A** No, she _____ .

④ **Q** 今日の放課後も図書室のそうじですか？

**Q** _____ you clean the library after school today?

**A** いいえ、図書室のそうじはしません。　　私たちは、校庭で野球をするつもりです。

**A** _____ , we _____ . We _____ play baseball in the school yard.

**4** **Write your own answers.**

① Was it sunny yesterday? _____

② Was it cold this morning? _____

③ Were you busy last Saturday? _____

④ Who was absent from English class last week? _____

⑤ When and where were you born? _____

⑥ Will it be hot tomorrow? _____

⑦ Is it hot today? _____

⑧ Are you busy today? _____

## 1 📖 Words / Phrases

| | | | | |
|---|---|---|---|---|
| 1 | problem ( ) _____ | | 10 | reduce ( ) _____ |
| 2 | can ( ) _____ | | 11 | reuse ( ) _____ |
| 3 | bottle ( ) _____ | | 12 | recycle ( ) _____ |
| 4 | plastic ( ) _____ | | 13 | garbage ( ) _____ |
| 5 | styrofoam ( ) _____ | | 14 | empty ( ) _____ |
| 6 | tray ( ) _____ | | 15 | metal ( ) _____ |
| 7 | throw away ( ) _____ | | 16 | egg shell ( ) _____ |
| 8 | again ( ) _____ | | 17 | instead of ( ) _____ |
| 9 | possible ( ) _____ | | 18 | fish bones ( ) _____ |

## 2 Rewrite the sentences using be going to.

**1** She plays catch with him.
_____
_____ tomorrow.

**2** They meet you at the station.
_____
_____ this afternoon.

**3** Nancy sends you a postcard.
_____
_____

**4** Does he wash his car?
_____
_____

**5** Do you call her?
_____
_____ tonight?

**6** Where do we meet her?
_____
_____

**3** | **Use answers from 2.** | ❶~❸ : **Rewrite the sentences into questions.** | ❶~❸: 2 の答えの英文を疑問文にしましょう。
| | ❹~❻ : **Answer the questions.** | ❹~❻: 2 の質問に答えましょう。

**1** _____

**2** _____

**3** _____

**4** Yes, _____ No, _____

**5** Yes, _____ No, _____

**6** _____ at a cafe near my house.

**4** **Make sentences that match the Japanese.**

**1** ランチに何を食べるつもりですか？
_____

**2** あなたはこのゴミをどうするつもりですか？ (this garbage)
_____

**3** あなたはこれらの缶を捨てるつもりですか？ (these cans)
_____

**4** あなたは今日の午後、トムとテニスをするつもりですか？
_____

**5** 彼女に何を買うつもりですか？
_____

**5** **Write your own answers.**

**1** What are you going to eat for supper tonight? _____

**2** What are you going to do tomorrow? _____

**3** How are you going home after this lesson? _____

**4** Are you going to do your homework tonight? _____

## 1 📖 Words/Phrases

| | | | |
|---|---|---|---|
| ① | grow up ( ) _____ | ⑨ | Venezuela ( ) _____ |
| ② | travel ( ) _____ | ⑩ | come back ( ) _____ |
| ③ | India ( ) _____ | ⑪ | have a rest ( ) _____ |
| ④ | Turkey ( ) _____ | ⑫ | around ( ) _____ |
| ⑤ | cave ( ) _____ | ⑬ | itinerary ( ) _____ |
| ⑥ | Algeria ( ) _____ | ⑭ | based on ( ) _____ |
| ⑦ | desert ( ) _____ | ⑮ | let me tell you ( ) _____ |
| ⑧ | Italy ( ) _____ | ⑯ | the funniest ( ) _____ |

## 2 Rewrite the sentences using appropriate form of verbs.

**1** He comes to see me.

_____ tomorrow.

**2** The bus comes here.

_____ in ten minutes.

**3** She is a doctor.

_____ in the future.

**4** She goes to a college in Tokyo.

_____ next year.

**5** They cook dinner for you.

_____ tonight.

**6** It is fine.

_____ this afternoon.

**7** It rains.

_____ now.

**2**

3 ❶~❸ : Rewrite the previous sentences using not.　❶~❸：2 で書いた答えの英文を否定文にしましょう。

❹~❼ : Rewrite the previous sentences into questions.　❹~❼：2 で書いた答えの英文を疑問文にしましょう。

**1**

**2**

**3**

**4**

**5**

**6**

**7**

○ Will は未来のことを表す時だけでなく、人に何か「お願いする」時にも使います。

☐ **Will you help me?　No problem.** 伝ってくれませんか？　いいとも。（問題ないです）

☐ **Will you come with me?　Sure!** 私と一緒に来てくれませんか？　もちろん！

4 **Put the words in order to make sentences that match the Japanese.**

① 窓をあけてくださいませんか？　　　　　(the / will /open / you / window)?

② ここでしばらくお待ちくださいますか？　(will / a moment / for / wait / you)?

③ 今夜、手伝いに来てくれませんか？　　　(come / help / to / me / you / tonight / will)?

④ 駅までの道を教えてくれませんか？　　　(tell / way / the / to / the station / you / me / will)?

5 **Write your own answers.**

Where will you live when you are twenty years old?

## 1 📖 Words / Phrases

① by yourself
(　　　　　) _____

② by myself
(　　　　　) _____

③ behave yourself
(　　　　　) _____

④ without
(　　　　　) _____

⑤ measure
(　　　　　) _____

⑥ be sure to
(　　　　　) _____

## 2 Put the words in order to make sentences that match the Japanese.

- ☐ too ...　　　…すぎる
- ☐ too ... to ～　　～するには…すぎる
　　　　　　　　　　（…すぎて～できない）
- ☐ ... enough to ～　　～するほど十分に…
- ☐ get along with ...　…とうまくやる
- ☐ May I ...?　　　…していいですか？

① 暑くて外で仕事できません。
(outside / work / It / too hot / to / is)

_____

② 私は十分そこに1人で行ける年齢です。
(enough / go / I am / by myself / old / there / to)

_____

③ このかばんを持ち上げられますか？ 私には重すぎます。
(lift / you / bag / can / this)?　(too / is / me / It / for / heavy)

_____

④ 質問をしていいですか？
(question / may / you / ask / a / I)?

_____

⑤ 新しい友達とうまくいっていますか？
How (along / getting / are / you / with) your new friends?

_____

⑥ このジェットコースターに乗るには君は年齢が若すぎる。
(too / young / ride / you / are / to / this ) roller coaster.

_____

⑦ 彼らは理解するにはあまりにも速く話します。
(fast / understand/ they /speak / too /to)

_____

⑧ 私は幸運にもそのチケットを手に入れることができた。
(the tickets / enough /to get / I / lucky / was)

_____

**3**

**3** **Read the sentences and write the questions and answers.** Why? と Because... の文章を作りましょう。

☐ **Why ...?  Because ....** なぜ～ですか？　なぜなら～です。

**①**
Jenny got up early. She had to go to school before 8 o'clock.

Why did Jenny get up early?

Because she had to _____

**②**
Rick studied English hard. He wanted to speak English well.

Why did Rick _____

Because he _____

**③**
Sue and Ken went to the department store. They wanted to buy a present for their mother.

_____
_____
_____
_____

**4** **Write your own answers.**

**1** Do you want to go to Hawaii?
_____
_____

**2** Do you think you are old enough to go to Hawaii by yourself?
_____
_____

**3** Do you want to fly in an airplane?
_____
_____

**4** Do you think you are too young to go to see movies only with friends?
_____
_____

**5** Can you get along with new people easily?
_____
_____

**6** Is an eighteen-year-old student old enough to leave home and live alone?
_____
_____

**7** What can you do by yourself?
_____
_____

## 1 📖 **Words / Phrases**

⑨～⑯ 三単現 s の形を書きましょう。

① treat
(        ) _____

② occupation
(        ) _____

③ program
(        ) _____

④ fiction
(        ) _____

⑤ television
(        ) _____

⑥ homework
(        ) _____

⑦ solid
(        ) _____

⑧ liquid
(        ) _____

⑨ use
( 使う ) _uses_____

⑩ lose
(        ) _____

⑪ choose
(        ) _____

⑫ catch
(        ) _____

⑬ teach
(        ) _____

⑭ become
(        ) _____

⑮ complete
(        ) _____

⑯ collect
(        ) _____

## 2 **Make sentences using the key words in the (        ) and write the Japanese.**

① That boy _____ a ticket to the concert. (have)  (                    )

② Cindy _____ the computer every day. (use)  (                    )

③ Bill's aunt _____ history at junior high school. (teach)
(                    )

④ Daisuke _____ home late every Friday. (come)  (                    )

⑤ Yuki _____ to a private elementary school. (go)  (                    )

⑥ Naomi _____ learning foreign languages. (like)  (                    )

⑦ Mr. Miller _____ four languages. (speak)  (                    )

**1**

## 3 Put the words in order to make sentences that match the Japanese.

**①** 日本では学校は4月から始まります。　　　　School ( in / in / begins / April / Japan ).

**②** 太陽は東からのぼります。　　　　The sun ( in / rises / east / the ).

**③** 太陽は私たちに光と熱を与えてくれます。　　　　The sun ( us / gives / and / light / heat ).

**④** 1年間は365日です。　　　　There ( three hundred sixty-five / are / in / a / days ) year.

## 4 Write your own answers.

**1** Does your father smoke?

**2** Does your teacher play golf?

**3** Does your school have a swimming pool?

**4** Does your grandmother live near your house?

**5** What time does your school begin in the morning?

## 5 Water: After reading the passage on p.23 of the textbook, write what you know about water.
テキストp.23 の英文を読んで、水の3つの形態について知り得ることを書きましょう。

# Unit 4 ❷

## 1 📖 Words/Phrases 次の語を過去形にしましょう。

| ① look ( ) looked | ⑪ feel ( ) | ㉑ break ( ) |
| ② climb ( ) | ⑫ say ( ) | ㉒ catch ( ) |
| ③ help ( ) | ⑬ think ( ) | ㉓ teach ( ) |
| ④ cook ( ) | ⑭ win ( ) | ㉔ speak ( ) |
| ⑤ want ( ) | ⑮ stand ( ) | ㉕ eat ( ) |
| ⑥ start ( ) | ⑯ wash ( ) | ㉖ pay ( ) |
| ⑦ crash ( ) | ⑰ try ( ) | ㉗ write ( ) |
| ⑧ walk ( ) | ⑱ stop ( ) | ㉘ make ( ) |
| ⑨ live ( ) | ⑲ read ( ) | ㉙ take ( ) |
| ⑩ play ( ) | ⑳ meet ( ) | ㉚ plan ( ) |

## 2 Rewrite the sentences using the past tense.

① I go to school early. ▷ _____

② I see many stars in the sky. ▷ _____

③ I take pictures with my friends. ▷ _____

④ I do my homework. ▷ _____

⑤ I go to bed at nine o'clock. ▷ _____

⑥ I say good-bye to my friend. ▷ _____

## 3 Rewrite the sentences using not.

1 I walked to school yesterday. ▷ _____

2 I made this doll for you. ▷ _____

3 I watched a baseball game on TV.
▷ _____

4 My mother and I ate sandwiches for lunch.
▷ _____

5 I saw a beautiful moon last night.
▷ _____

## 4 Write your own answers.

1 Did you brush your teeth this morning?
_____

2 Did you take a bath last night?
_____

3 Did you go to school the day before yesterday?
_____

4 What time did you go home yesterday?
_____

5 How did you come here today?
_____

6 What time did you go to bed last night?
_____

7 How many hours did you sleep last night?
_____

8 Did you do your homework last night?
_____

## 1 📖 Words/Phrases

1. fail ( ) _____
2. aloud ( ) _____
3. word ( ) _____
4. sentence ( ) _____
5. memorize ( ) _____
6. feed the fish ( ) _____
7. salad ( ) _____
8. water the flowers ( ) _____
9. fold ( ) _____
10. laundry ( ) _____
11. household ( ) _____
12. vacuum ( ) _____
13. knew ( ) _____
14. found ( ) _____
15. bought ( ) _____
16. went ( ) _____

## 2 Rewrite the sentences using the past tense.

1. I take some pictures. _____
2. We see a lot of flowers in the park. _____
3. You write a long letter to your aunt. _____
4. Tina and I go shopping. _____
5. Daichi catches a cold. _____
6. Sally breaks the promise. _____
7. The lion drinks a lot of water. _____
8. We read many books in the library. _____

**3**

**3** Rewrite the previous sentences into questions.

1

2

3

4

5

6

7

8

**4** Choose one person from the textbook p.27 and write what he/she did and didn't do.

**5** Write three things you do to get good marks on English tests.

## 1 📖 Words / Phrases

⑧ 〜 ⑭ は過去形を書きましょう。

① alone
(          ) _____

② scary
(          ) _____

③ airport
(          ) _____

④ look forward to
(          ) _____

⑤ ceremony
(          ) _____

⑥ one-day trip
(          ) _____

⑦ uncle
(          ) _____

⑧ stay
(          ) _____

⑨ arrive at
(          ) _____

⑩ visit
(          ) _____

⑪ see
(          ) _____

⑫ leave
(          ) _____

⑬ have
(          ) _____

⑭ take a trip
(          ) _____

## 2 Complete the sentences using the correct form of the verb in ( ). （　）内の語を適当な形に変えて書きましょう。

① My uncle _____ the book now. (read)

② I _____ the same book one month ago. (read)

③ I _____ _____ the book again after my uncle. (read)

④ I _____ the report last night. (write)

⑤ David _____ me how to ride a bike yesterday. (teach)

⑥ My parents _____ in Hiroshima now. (be)

⑦ They are _____ _____ _____ for Izumo Taisha tomorrow. (leave)

⑧ Tadashi _____ a bath every day. (take)

⑨ He _____ a bath now. (take)

⑩ Jack _____ down the tree three years ago. (cut)

**3** Complete the sentences using the correct form of **go.**   go を正しい形に変えて入れましょう。

(1) I _____ to school with my friend every day.

(2) But I _____ _____ to school on Sundays.

(3) I _____ _____ to school now.

(4) My sister Tomoko _____ to junior high school.

(5) Tomoko _____ to school on foot.

(6) Tomoko _____ _____ _____ to school by train.

(7) I _____ _____ to the same junior high school next year.

(8) My sister and I _____ _____ to school together from next year.

**4** You are in the hotel. It is eight o'clock in the morning on September 8th.
According to the itinerary on textbook p.29, write what you **did** and what you **will do.**

## 1 📖 Words/Phrases

| ① large | ( 大きい ) | larger | largest |
|---|---|---|---|
| ② easy | ( ) | | |
| ③ pretty | ( ) | | |
| ④ good | ( ) | | |
| ⑤ well | ( ) | | |
| ⑥ bad | ( ) | | |
| ⑦ interesting | ( ) | | |
| ⑧ difficult | ( ) | | |
| ⑨ warm | ( ) | | |
| ⑩ popular | ( ) | | |
| ⑪ fast | ( ) | | |
| ⑫ nice | ( ) | | |
| ⑬ cheap | ( ) | | |
| ⑭ expensive | ( ) | | |

○「比較級を強める」時は、**much**を使います。

**This is much easier.** もっと簡単な　**This movie is much more interesting.** もっとずっとおもしろい

## 2 Complete the sentences using the correct form of the word ( ). （　）内の語を適する形にしましょう。

① It is much _____ this year than last year. (cold)

② I feel much _____ today than yesterday. (good)

③ January is the _____ month of the year in Australia. (hot)

④ You look _____ in a white shirt than in a red one. (pretty)

⑤ Some of my classmates knew _____ about Japanese history than I did. (much)

⑥ This train runs much _____ than that one. (fast)

⑦ Please speak a little _____ slowly. (much)

**3 Circle the correct words in the (  ) and make sentences.**

① This camera is the ( much,  more,  most,  very ) expensive one in this store.

② Lake Biwa is larger than any ( lakes,  other lakes,  other lake ) in Japan.

③ Who came to school the ( more early,  earlier,  earliest ) in this class?

④ Taro is the tallest ( in,  of,  with,  from ) all the boys in his class.

⑤ Mike is the ( good,   better,  best ) athlete in our school.

⑥ What is the ( popular,  popularest,  most popular ) transportation in Japan?

⑦ I like autumn ( much,  better,  the best ) of the four seasons.

⑧ Nancy is the ( tallest,  tall,  taller ) of the children.

**4 Answer the following questions in English.**

① What is the second largest island in Japan?

② Which do you like better, math or science?

③ Which is the coldest month in Japan?

④ Who is the strongest teacher in your school?

⑤ Which is farther from Japan, the Antarctic or the Arctic?

(the Antarctic = South Pole,  the Arctic = North Pole)

## 1 📖 Words / Phrases

**1** field
( )  _____

**2** huge
( )  _____

**3** country
( )  _____

**4** grass
( )  _____

**5** finally
( )  _____

**6** pop
( )  _____

**7** all the way home
( )  _____

**8** puff up
( )  _____

**9** take a breath
( )  _____

**10** Russia
( )  _____

**11** Germany
( )  _____

**12** almost
( )  _____

**13** size
( )  _____

**14** therefore
( )  _____

A is **as** big **as** B.    A は B と同じくらい大きい。

## 2 Complete the sentences to match the Japanese.

**1** この家はあの家と同じくらい古い。

This house is _____ old _____ that house.

**2** 私の父は私と同じくらいの背の高さです。

My father is as _____ _____ I am.

**3** 彼は私と同じくらい本を持っています。

He has as _____ _____ as I have.

**4** 弟はぼくの2倍食べる。

My brother eats _____ _____ _____ I do.

**5** この問題は私が思ったほどむずかしくありません。

This problem is not _____ difficult _____ I thought.

**6** 白雪姫の肌は雪のように白く、唇はバラのように赤く、髪は黒檀のように黒かった。

Snow White's skin was (as) _____ as _____ , her lips were (as) _____ _____

a rose, and her hair was (as) _____ _____ ebony.

**3** **Read the story of The Cow and the Frog on p.32 of the textbook and answer the questions.**

**1** What was the cow eating?

**2** Where was the cow?

**3** Why was the little frog very surprised?

**4** Where did the little frog go?

**5** Who did the little frog tell about the huge animal?

**6** What did the mother frog do to puff herself up?

**7** Was the mother frog smaller than the cow?

**8** Could the mother frog become bigger than a basketball?

**9** Could the mother frog become as big as a cat?

**10** Could the mother frog become as big as a horse?

**11** Could the mother frog become bigger than a dog?

**12** Could the mother frog become as big as the cow?

**4** **Write your own answers.**

**1** If you could be an animal, what animal would you want to be?

**2** Why?

## 1 📖 Words / Phrases

1. stop by ( ) _____
2. convenience ( ) _____
3. else ( ) _____
4. borrow ( ) _____
5. school uniform ( ) _____
6. during ( ) _____
7. bow ( ) _____
8. dye ( ) _____
9. earrings ( ) _____
10. modify ( ) _____
11. regularly ( ) _____
12. reasonable ( ) _____
13. acceptable ( ) _____
14. agree ( ) _____
15. on the way ( ) _____
16. regulation ( ) _____

## 2 Use the phrases below and complete the sentences. （同じものを何度選んでもかまいません）

1. あなたにお会いできてうれしいです。 I am glad _____ you.
2. おばあさんは川へせんたくに行きました。 The old lady went to the river _____ the clothes.
3. 私は買い物に行きたくありません。 I don't want _____ shopping.
4. 私は何か食べるものがほしい。 I want something _____ .
5. 私は放課後にすることがない。 I have nothing _____ after school.
6. 私の両親は私に勉強してほしいと思っています。 My parents want me _____ .
7. それを聞いてうれしいです。 I am glad _____ that.
8. 私は、今日は宿題をしたくない。 I don't want _____ my homework today.

to do    to study    to go    to eat    to meet    to wash    to hear

**3** **Translate the sentences into Japanese.**

不定詞に下線を引き、不定詞が修飾しているものを○で囲み、全文の意味を書きましょう。

**Ex.** What is the best (way) to learn English?　(英語で学習する一番良い方法は何でしょうか。)

① There is no clean water to drink in this area. (　　　　　　　　　　　　　　　)

② Mr. and Mrs. Smith had to find someone to take care of their baby.

(　　　　　　　　　　　　　　　　　　　　　　　　　　　　　　)

③ I'm looking for a place to stay in Nara. (　　　　　　　　　　　　　　　　　)

○ 「…することは（人にとって）～です」

**It is ～（for人）to …**　　**It is easy ( for me ) to answer the question.**
その質問に答えることは私にとって簡単です。

**4** **Put the words in order to make sentences that match the Japanese.**

① その川を飛びこえることは彼にとって簡単でした。　It was easy ( for / jump over / to / the river / him ).

② 私がその問題を解くなんて不可能です。　It is impossible ( for / to / the problem / me / solve ).

③ 私は、今夜は疲れすぎてお風呂に入れません。　I am too tired ( take / to / bath / a ) tonight.

④ このスープは熱くて飲めません。　This soup is ( too / eat / hot / to).

⑤ 相互理解を持つことは重要です。　It is important ( to / understanding / have / mutual ).

⑥ ぼくの父はその新しい家を買わないことを決めました。　My father decided ( to / the / house / buy / not / new ).

⑦ その自転車は高価すぎてぼくには買えません。　The bicycle is ( for / me / to / buy / expensive / too ).

# 1 📖 Words/Phrases

| | | | | |
|---|---|---|---|---|
| ① | listen to me ( ) | _____ | ⑦ | positive ( ) | _____ |
| ② | leave me alone ( ) | _____ | ⑧ | negative ( ) | _____ |
| ③ | study hard ( ) | _____ | ⑨ | the elderly ( ) | _____ |
| ④ | while ( ) | _____ | ⑩ | university ( ) | _____ |
| ⑤ | offer ( ) | _____ | ⑪ | in the future ( ) | _____ |
| ⑥ | attitude ( ) | _____ | ⑫ | diary ( ) | _____ |

**want …** …がほしい  **want to …** …したい  **want 人 to …** （人）に…してもらいたい

# 2 Compare two sentences and put them into Japanese.

**1**
I want to go there and see him. ( )
I want you to go there and see him. ( )

**2**
My mother wanted to take a bath. ( )
My mother wanted me to take a bath. ( )

**3**
I want to write a letter to apologize. ( )
I want you to write a letter to apologize. ( )

**4**
My parents want to be famous. ( )
My parents want me to be famous. ( )

**3** **Make sentences that match the Japanese.**

**1** 私は自分の部屋をきれいにしたい。
_____

**2** 私はあなたに自分の部屋をきれいにしてもらいたい。
_____

**3** 私はこの本を読みたい。
_____

**4** 私はあなたにこの本を読んでもらいたい。
_____

**5** 私はあなたの隣にすわりたい。
_____

**6** 私はあなたに私の隣にすわってほしくない。
_____

**7** 私は海外で勉強しようと決めました。 (overseas)
I decided _____

**8** 私は海外で勉強しないことに決めました。
I decided _____

**9** 彼は私に手紙を書くと約束しました。
He promised _____

**10** 彼は2度と遅刻をしないと約束しました。 (be late)
He promised _____

**4** **Write your own answers using –er or more.**

**1** I want to be _____ (more / -er)

**2** I want my English teacher to be _____ (more / -er)

**3** I want (my mother / my father) to be _____ (more / -er)

## 1 📖 Words / Phrases

1 I told you （ 　　　） _____

2 everything （ 　　　） _____

3 museum （ 　　　） _____

4 go surfing （ 　　　） _____

5 go skiing （ 　　　） _____

6 aquarium （ 　　　） _____

7 concert hall （ 　　　） _____

8 shopping mall （ 　　　） _____

9 what to do （ 　　　） _____

10 where to go （ 　　　） _____

11 when to go （ 　　　） _____

12 how to go （ 　　　） _____

13 get off （ 　　　） _____

14 stranger （ 　　　） _____

15 ticket （ 　　　） _____

16 get there （ 　　　） _____

## 2 Put the words in order to make sentences that match the Japanese.

1 Will you show me (this / how / use / machine / to)? 　　この機械の使い方

_____

2 We should decide (buy / for / to / what / her). 　　彼女のために買うもの

_____

3 Tell me (to / where / start). 　　どこから始める（のか）

_____

4 I don't know (way / to / which / take). 　　どの道を行けばいい（のか）

_____

5 Will you tell me (contact / to / how / him)? 　　彼にどのように連絡を取ればよい（のか）

_____

# Cambridge English

# ヤングラーナーズ英語検定（YLE）とは

ケンブリッジ大学のグループ機関の一つである、ケンブリッジ大学英語検定機構によって開発されたテストです。ヤングラーナーズ英語検定（YLE）は、スターターズ、ムーバーズ、フライヤーズの３つのレベルから成るテストで、Cambridge English（ケンブリッジ英語検定）の第一歩にあたります。
楽しく英語を学びながら効果的に「読む」「書く」「話す」「聞く」の４つの技能をバランスよく伸ばせるよう工夫されているので、楽しんで受けることができる試験です。
楽しみながら、世界で通用するケンブリッジ英語検定への準備が一歩一歩着実にできる YLE テストで確かな英語力と自信を育てましょう。

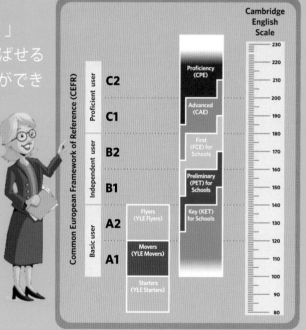

## リスニングテストでは：

・音声は２回流れます。もし１回目で聞き逃しても、もう一度聞くチャンスがあります。
・上手に色がぬってあるか、絵が上手に描けているかは重要ではありません。指示通りの色で正しいものをぬっているか、指示されたものとわかる絵が描かれているかが重要です。

## リーディング＆ライティングテストでは：

・採点者がはっきり分かるように答えを書いているか確認しましょう。
・ほとんどの場合、答えはとても短く、数字を英語で書いたり、単語で答える際は選択肢や文中から書き写す問題が多いので、文章で答える必要はありません。

## スピーキングテストでは：

・試験官は協力的で話しやすい雰囲気を作ってくれます。また、経験が豊富なので受験する皆さんの力をうまく引き出してくれます。だから、皆さんはリラックスしてスピーキングテストを楽しめるはず！
'Good morning' 'Pardon?' 'Yes, please' 'Thank you' など、いつも使っているフレーズをなるべく使うように心がけるとよいでしょう。
・もし言われたことが理解できなかった場合は、質問を繰り返してほしいとお願いすることができます。次の表現がすらっと言えるとよいですね。

## Listening

# Part 1

**– 5 questions –**

**Listen and draw lines. There is one example.**

Fred          Paul          Jim          Jane

Sally          Peter          Vicky

# Part 2
### – 5 questions –

**Listen and write. There is one example.**

## Shopping in the supermarket

Goes shopping:                  in the ............ morning ............

1   Likes shop because:       It's always .....................................

2   Every day buys:                  .....................................

3   Comes to the supermarket by:     .....................................

4   Comes shopping with:        his .....................................

5   Name:                       Mr .....................................

# Part 3

## – 5 questions –

**What did Jack do last week?**

**Listen and draw a line from the day to the correct picture.**

**There is one example.**

Monday

Tuesday

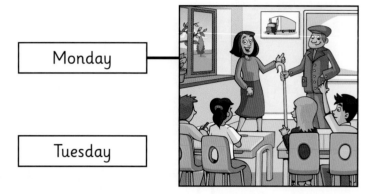

Wednesday

Thursday

Friday

Saturday

Sunday

# Part 4
### – 5 questions –

## Listen and tick (✔) the box. There is one example.

What's John doing now?

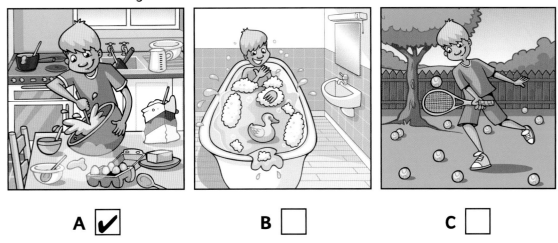

A ✔  B ☐  C ☐

1    Which clown does Daisy like most?

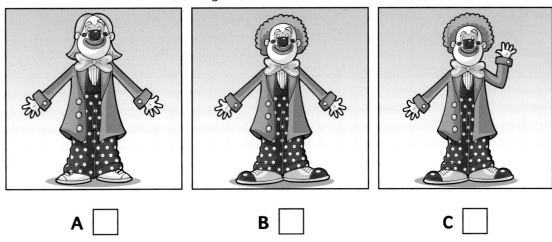

A ☐  B ☐  C ☐

2    What did Tony dream about?

A ☐  B ☐  C ☐

3    What does Ben need?

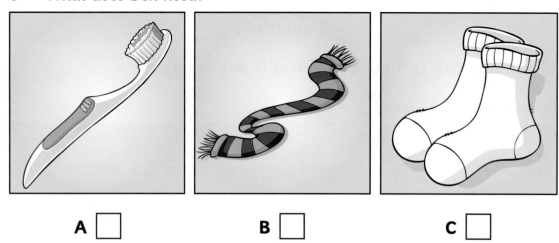

A ☐              B ☐              C ☐

4    Where's Pat's favourite CD?

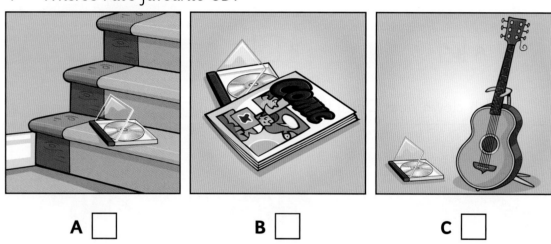

A ☐              B ☐              C ☐

5    Which is Kim's puppy?

A ☐              B ☐              C ☐

# Part 5
## – 5 questions –

**Listen and colour and draw. There is one example.**

## Reading and Writing

# Part 1

### – 6 questions –

Look and read. Choose the correct words and write them on the lines. There is one example.

a jungle

lakes

flowers

a monkey

a market

grass

a giraffe

a school

## Example

Children learn and have lessons here.              ............... *a school* ...............

## Questions

1    You see these in gardens, parks and
     sometimes houses.                              ...................................

2    This animal is good at climbing and can
     hold things.                                   ...................................

3    You can buy your food and clothes in
     this place.                                    ...................................

4    This place has a lot of trees and plants.      ...................................

5    This animal is very tall and has a long
     neck.                                          ...................................

6    This is green. You can walk or sit on it.      ...................................

# Part 2

### – 6 questions –

**Look and read. Write yes or no.**

## Examples

A dog is playing with a ball. ..................yes...................

All the baby's clothes are yellow. ..................no...................

## Questions

1   Two dolphins are swimming and one is jumping.

.....................................

2   The woman in the blue T-shirt has longer hair than the woman in the red T-shirt.

.....................................

3   The weather is wet and we can see a rainbow.

.....................................

4   The boy who is wearing a hat is eating a sandwich.

.....................................

5   A man is giving some fish to two cats.

.....................................

6   A woman with grey hair is pointing to an elephant.

.....................................

# Part 3
## – 6 questions –

**Read the text and choose the best answer.**

### Example

**Sally:**      Hello, Jill. Did you have a good weekend?

**Jill:**       A    Yes, I have.
               B    Yes, thank you.
               C    Yes, she did.

### Questions

1   **Sally:**      Did you ride your horse?

    **Jill:**       A    Yes, it did.
                   B    Yes, I did.
                   C    Yes, he did.

2 **Sally:** How often do you go riding?

   **Jill:**    A   I go to the forest.
                  B   I go with my sister.
                  C   I go every evening.

3 **Jill:** Would you like to come and see my horse on Saturday?

   **Sally:**   A   Yes, I like it.
                  B   Yes, I'd like that.
                  C   Yes, it's like a horse.

4 **Sally:** Where is your horse?

   **Jill:**    A   It's in a field near the park.
                  B   It's big and brown.
                  C   Its name is Cloud.

5 **Sally:** Have you got pets at home?

   **Jill:**    A   Yes, I have two mice.
                  B   Yes, they live at the zoo.
                  C   Yes, they've got three.

6 **Sally:** Oh! Here's my bus! I've got to go now.

   **Jill:**    A   No, let's go home!
                  B   Yes, that's right!
                  C   OK, see you!

# Part 4
### – 7 questions –

**Read the story. Choose a word from the box. Write the correct word next to numbers 1–6. There is one example.**

On the first day of John and Jim's school holidays they cleaned their

.............. *bikes* .............. and then rode them to the village shop. They

wanted to go to the **(1)** ..................... for the day and they

needed some food to take with them.

The boys looked around the shop. They bought bread, cheese

and two ice creams. But then a young girl in the shop hurt her

**(2)** ..................... when she dropped a small bottle on it. Jim

said, "Don't **(3)** ..................... !" and John said, "Here, have

my ice cream."

Then a woman shouted, "Look! There's a spider in that

**(4)** ..................... of mangoes!" and she ran out. Some people

were **(5)** ..................... of the spider, but Jim caught it in his

hands, **(6)** ..................... it outside and put it on the ground.

Then the man who worked in the shop said, "Thank you, boys!" and he

gave them both the biggest ice creams in the shop.

### Example

| | | |
|---|---|---|
| bikes | box | river |
| hungry | foot | carried |
| smile | cry | afraid |

**(7) Now choose the best name for the story.**

**Tick one box.**

Two men go shopping ☐

Two boys help some people ☐

Two friends ride to the school ☐

# Part 5
### – 10 questions –

**Look at the pictures and read the story. Write some words to complete the sentences about the story. You can use 1, 2 or 3 words. There are two examples.**

## The birthday pirate

Last weekend, Bill, Jane and their parents went to the sea for Bill's birthday. It was sunny at the beach. The children played badminton with their father. Mum put a picnic on a red blanket. The family sat on the blanket and ate their lunch. They gave Bill a cake and they sang a birthday song. After their food, Mum and Dad slept.

## Examples

On the day that the family went to the beach, the weather was
..................... sunny ..................... .

Bill, Jane and ..................... their father ..................... played badminton.

## Questions

1    When they ate their picnic at the beach, they sat on

..................................... .

2    ..................................... went to sleep after lunch.

The children were not tired. They wanted to play in the sea. Jane jumped and ran in the water and Bill played with his toy boat. He thought, "I'd like to sail on a big boat."

Then they saw a pirate! He had a green parrot on his shoulder.

3   Jane and Bill played in ..................................... .

4   ..................................... had a toy boat.

5   Bill wanted to ..................................... on a boat.

6   The pirate had a ..................................... with him.

The pirate said, "Hello! Would you like a ride in my boat?" The children said, "Yes, please!"

The pirate took them to an island. They climbed trees and played. The pirate gave them some coconuts, which they ate at the top of the trees. Then he said, "I must take you back to your parents." Bill said, "That was the best birthday! Thank you!"

When they went back to the beach, their parents were awake. They talked to the pirate and gave him a cup of tea.

7    Bill and Jane went in the boat with the pirate to

     ..................................... .


8    They ate ..................................... up the trees.


9    On the beach their mum and dad were ..................................... .


10   The pirate had some ..................................... with Mum and Dad.

## Part 6
– 5 questions –

**Read the text. Choose the right words and write them on the lines.**

## Bananas

**Example**   Bananas .............. are .............. a kind of fruit. A lot of people in

the world eat bananas.

We can buy bananas in shops. They are from banana trees

1   .............................. hot countries.

2   These trees .............................. very big leaves and they need a

lot of water.

People take the bananas off the trees. Then they

3   .............................. them and put them on planes and then the

bananas go to other countries.

4   People often eat yellow bananas and ..............................

5   people eat green bananas .............................. they cook

like fries.

|  |  |  |  |  |
|---|---|---|---|---|
| **Example** | | is | are | am |
| 1 | | on | in | at |
| 2 | | have | has | had |
| 3 | | washes | washing | wash |
| 4 | | every | some | any |
| 5 | | which | what | who |

# ムーバーズ・スピーキングテスト (Movers)

ムーバーズ・スピーキングのテスト概要、問題サンプル、実際のテストの様子です。

テスト概要

| スピーキング 5-7 分 | 1 | 2 枚の絵を見て違いを見つける（物、色、数、場所など） | 何が違うか述べる |
|---|---|---|---|
| | 2 | 4 枚から成る絵を見てそのストーリーを話す | 短い文章で答える |
| | 3 | 4 枚の絵から仲間はずれを 1 枚選ぶ | その一枚がどのように異なっているのか話す |
| | 4 | 自分自身について答える | 簡潔に答える |

ストーリー問題のサンプル

仲間はずれ問題とテスト風景

# ヤングラーナーズ（YLE）公式問題集

OFFICIAL

## Cambridge English Young Learners 1 for Revised Exam from 2018

NEW

Starters     Movers     Flyers

2018 年テスト改訂版対応教材

## Cambridge English Young Learners 9

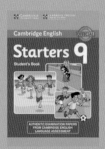

Starters     Movers     Flyers

ケンブリッジ英検対策本の問い合わせは：

ケンブリッジ大学出版株式会社　ELT

Email: japanelt@cambridge.org

www.cambridge.org/elt

試験についてのお問い合わせは：

ケンブリッジ大学英語検定機構

Email: InfoJapan@cambridgeenglishreps.org

www.cambridgeenglish.org/jp

○ ～（人）に…するように言う（**tell**）

- ☐ **He told me to read this book.** 彼は 私に この本を 読むように 言いました。
- ☐ **He told me not to read this book.** 彼は 私に この本を 読まないように 言いました。

● このような言い方をする主な動詞に次のようなものがあります。

**ask ～ to …** （～に…するように頼む）　　　　**advise ～ to …** （～に…するように助言する）

**3** **Translate the sentences into Japanese.**

**1** He asked me to open the window.

(　　　　　　　　　　　　　　　　　　　　　　　　　　　　　　　　　　)

**2** He asked me not to open the window.

(　　　　　　　　　　　　　　　　　　　　　　　　　　　　　　　　　　)

**4** **Complete the sentences to match the Japanese.**

**1** 彼に、私に電話をかけ直すようにお伝えください。

Please tell him to _____ _____ _____

**2** 母は私に帰りにいくつか卵を買ってくるように頼みました。

My mother asked me to _____ _____ _____ on the way home.

**3** 姫はその箱を開けてはいけないと言いました。

The princess told me _____ _____ _____ the box.

**4** ぼくの先生はぼくに、もっと英語を勉強するように言います。

My teacher tells me _____ _____ _____ _____

**5** **Write your own answers.**

**1** Do you know how to say thank you in five different languages?

_____
_____

**2** Do you know where to find beetles?

_____
_____

**3** Do you know how to set up the computer?

_____
_____

**4** I want to learn how to _____

## 1 📖 Words / Phrases

| № | Word | | № | Word | |
|---|---|---|---|---|---|
| 1 | advice ( ) | _____ | 8 | straight ( ) | _____ |
| 2 | script ( ) | _____ | 9 | clearly ( ) | _____ |
| 3 | prepare ( ) | _____ | 10 | loudly ( ) | _____ |
| 4 | practice ( ) | _____ | 11 | friendly ( ) | _____ |
| 5 | confident ( ) | _____ | 12 | important ( ) | _____ |
| 6 | audience ( ) | _____ | 13 | give a speech ( ) | _____ |
| 7 | website ( ) | _____ | 14 | fever ( ) | _____ |

### アドバイスの語彙

strong expressions ———————————————————————— mild expressions

**must** — **had better** — **should** — **have to** — **have got to**

***Suggestions***: If I were you …, I would …    Why don't you …?

## 2 Translate the sentences into Japanese.

① You must take off your shoes here. ( )

② You had better wait and see. ( )

③ You had better not eat too much junk food. ( )

④ You should stand straight and keep your head up. ( )

⑤ Do I have to call you before I go? ( )

⑥ I had to wait for more than one hour. ( )

⑦ If I were you, I'd practice reading the script in front of a mirror.
( )

**3** **Rewrite the sentences to match the Japanese.**　　次の文を（　　）の指示に従って書き直しましょう。

**1** You should leave the door open.　　(するべきではない)

**2** I have to pay for it.　　(yesterday を付けて)

**3** You had better take a bath today.　　(〜しない方がよい)

**4** You must speak loudly here.　　(〜してはならない)

**5** We have to go to school.　　(tomorrowを付けて、〜する必要はない)

**6** We have to clean our classroom.　　(疑問文に)

**4** **Write in both English and Japanese what you have to do to give a good speech.**

## 1 📖 Words / Phrases

| | | | |
|---|---|---|---|
| ① | get lost ( ) _____ | ⑥ | thousand ( ) _____ |
| ② | take bus No.4 ( ) _____ | ⑦ | signature ( ) _____ |
| ③ | length ( ) _____ | ⑧ | do nothing ( ) _____ |
| ④ | tunnel ( ) _____ | ⑨ | shake hands ( ) _____ |
| ⑤ | donate ( ) _____ | ⑩ | per second ( ) _____ |

○ 「If ... もしも…とすると」

A: 「起こりうる『もしも』と それに続いて起こること」　　If you press this button,
↓
the door will open.

B: 「想像される『もしも』と、 その結果起こるだろうと思われること」　　If I pressed this button,
↓
a monster would appear.

## 2 Translate the sentences into Japanese.

**A:** 「起こりうる『もしも』とそれに続いて起こること」

① If it is fine, we will go out to play. ( )

② If you are free, will you help me? ( )

③ If you know the results, please tell me. ( )

④ If you go, I will go too. ( )

⑤ If you have some eggs, I will make you an omelet. ( )

⑥ If you are seventy years or older, you don't have to pay the fee. ( )

**B:** 「想像される『もしも』と、その結果起こるだろうと思われること」

① If it stopped raining, we could go out to play. ( )

② If I won the lottery, I would buy a yacht. ( )

③ If I were free, I would be very happy to go and see you.

(                                                                    )

④ If I knew, I would tell you, but I don't.

(                                                                    )

**C:** 「今はできないけれど〜だったらいいのになあ」

① I wish I could go with you.    (                                    )

② I wish you were here.    (                                    )

**D:** 「もし、きみの立場だったら〜するのになあ」

① If I were you, I would not do such a thing.    (                        )

② If I were you, I would stay home.    (                              )

**3** **Answer the following questions.**

① It is 1.5 kilometers from my house to my school. If I walk 50 meters per minute, how long does it take me to go to school on foot?

_____
_____
_____

② There is a building that is 10 meters wide. If I plant a tree every two meters in front of the building, how many trees do I need?

_____
_____
_____

**4** **Complete the sentences to match the Japanese.**

① I wish I _____ his phone number.　　　彼の電話番号を知っていたらなあ。

② I wish I _____ _____ Chinese better.　　　もっと上手に中国語を話すことができればなあ。

③ I wish I _____ go to New York again.　　　もう一度ニューヨークに行けたらなあ。

④ If you _____ a queen, what would you do?　　　もし女王だったら何をする？

⑤ If I _____ money with me, I would lend you some.　　　もしお金を持っていたら君に貸してあげるのに。

## ① 📖 Words / Phrases

1. show ( )  _____
2. as you know ( )  _____
3. favorite ( )  _____
4. toy ( )  _____
5. birthday ( )  _____

6. decide ( )  _____
7. mean ( )  _____
8. truth ( )  _____
9. donkey ( )  _____
10. give ( )  _____

---

○（人）に…を～する

☐ **He showed** me a picture.    彼は 私に 絵を 見せました。

☐ **He teaches** us history.    彼は 私たちに 歴史を 教えます。

●このような言い方をする主な動詞に次のようなものがあります。

**give, buy, lend, write, send, bring, tell, make**

**Ex.** Please send me a letter. He brought me beautiful roses. I gave him chocolate.

---

## ② Write sentences putting the words in ( ) in the correct place, and translate them into Japanese.

1. My father gave a nice camera. (me)    (    )
   _____

2. Miss Brian taught English. (us)    (    )
   _____

3. Please show the way to the library. (me)    (    )
   _____

4. Will you tell your phone number? (him)    (    )
   _____

5. Please write a letter. (her)    (    )
   _____

6. The police showed how to get there. (me) (    )
   _____

**7** Ibuki named Brownie. (her dog) ( )

**8** Please call Ben. (me) ( )

**3** **Put the words in order to make sentences that match the Japanese.**

① 直美は彼女に1か月に1度手紙を書きます。

(once / writes / her / a month / Naomi / a letter)

② 私に何か温かい飲み物を持ってきてください。

(please / something / to drink / bring / hot / me)

③ 店員は私に青いシャツを選んでくれました。

(me / a / the clerk / shirt / blue / chose)

④ その書類を速達で彼に送ってください。

(him / the paper / send / please) by express.

⑤ その本は私に大切な教訓を教えてくれました。

(me / that / book / important / taught / an / lesson)

⑥ ジョンにサッカーのスコアの付け方を教えてくれませんか？

(will / teach / keep score / how to / you / in soccer / John)

**4** **Read the story on p.44 of the textbook and answer the questions.**

**1** What is Ibuki's good friend? (What did she think it was?)

**2** Who gave her that?

**3** On what occasion did Ibuki receive it?

**4** In truth, what is it?

## 1 📖 Words / Phrases

① bright ( ) _____

② against ( ) _____

③ chase ( ) _____

④ appear ( ) _____

⑤ west ( ) _____

⑥ east ( ) _____

○ **動詞＋ing** で、今していることを付け加えて人や物をより詳しく言います。

**a dog** 犬

**a sleeping dog** 寝ている犬

**a dog sleeping on the bench** ベンチの上で寝ている犬

1語で説明する時は人や物の直前に、2語以上で説明する時は直後に置きます。

## 2 Circle the noun being described, and translate the phrases / sentences into Japanese.

**Ex.** a big (cow)　a (cow) eating grass

名詞を○で囲み、それを修飾している語句に下線を引いて日本語にしましょう。

1 the tall boy ( )

2 the boiling water ( )

3 the shooting star ( )

4 the boy in my class ( )

5 the bus for the city hall ( )

6 the boy wearing a red shirt ( )

7 the cat chasing a squirrel ( )

8 the men working in this company ( )

9 The man living in front of us has a big fishing boat.
( )

10 There are a lot of people waiting for the bus.
( )

**3** **Write phrases/sentences that match the Japanese, using the words in (    ).**

（    ）内の英語を入れる場所に∧を入れて全文を書きましょう。

① the girl　笑っている女の子

(smiling)

② the train　乗客で満員の電車

(full of passengers)

③ the building　私たちの学校の反対側にある建物

(across from our school)

④ the man　その木の横に立っている男性

(standing by the tree)

⑤ the boy　1列目に座っている背の高い男の子

(tall / sitting in the first row)

⑥ the man　その車から出てきた老人

(getting out of the car / old)

⑦ the train　神戸と東京の間を走る電車

(running between Kobe and Tokyo)

⑧ Do you know the man?　あなたのお母さんと話している男性を知っていますか？

(talking with your mother)

⑨ The man is our teacher.　ベンチの上で寝ている男性は私たちの先生です。

(sleeping on the bench)

⑩ That man is an actor.　むこうでコーヒーを飲んでいる背の高い男性は有名な俳優です。

(drinking coffee over there / tall / famous)

**4** **Venus:** After reading the passage on p. 47 of the textbook, write what you know about Venus.

テキストp.47の英文を読んで金星についてわかったことを書きましょう。

## 1 📖 Words / Phrases

① princess (          ) _____

② dwarf (          ) _____

③ poisoned (          ) _____

④ carriage (          ) _____

⑤ pheasant (          ) _____

⑥ save (          ) _____

⑦ castle (          ) _____

⑧ parents (          ) _____

○ 英語では1語で人や物を修飾（限定）する場合は、人や物のすぐ「前」に、2語以上で人や物を説明する場合はすぐ「後ろ」に付けます。

a tall  boy

a tall  boy  in our class

a tall  boy  running over there

a tall  boy  who speaks English

a tall  boy  (whom) everyone knows

a  bird  which I love so much

a  bird  which is singing

## 2 Circle the noun being described, and translate the phrases into Japanese.

**Ex.**　a yellow (bag)　　a (bag) on the desk　　名詞を〇で囲み、それを修飾している語句に下線を引いて日本語にしましょう。

① the beautiful sunset (                    )

② a comfortable chair (                    )

③ a huge black cloud (                    )

④ the cat running over there (                    )

⑤ a hotel near the airport (                    )

⑥ the girl talking with her friends (                    )

⑦ the teacher who teaches us English (                    )

⑧ the bus which goes to Tokyo (                    )

⑨ the book which you bought yesterday (                    )

⑩ the letter which you sent me (                    )

**11** I found a hotel which offers free Wi-Fi. ( )

**12** I have a friend whose first name is the same as mine. ( )

**3** **Write sentences that match the Japanese, using the words in (   ).**
（　　）内の語句が入る場所に∧を入れ、全文を書きましょう。

① その背の高い女性は私の先生です。　(tall)

The lady is my teacher. _____

② 私の母と話している背の高い女性は私の先生です。　(who is talking with my mother / tall)

The lady is my teacher. _____

③ だれか英語を話す人を探さなければいけません。　(who speaks English)

We have to look for someone. _____

④ その机の上にある黄色のかばんは私のものです。　(on the desk / yellow)

The bag is mine. _____

⑤ 高田行きのバスは17番です。　(which goes to Takada)

The bus is No. 17. _____

⑥ この学校を建てた人は木田博士です。　(who founded this school)

The man is Dr. Kida. _____

⑦ ケイトが今日着ているジャケットはとてもかわいいね。　(Kate is wearing today)

The jacket is very cute. _____

⑧ 私の母が焼いたケーキはとてもおいしい。　(my mother baked)

The cake is very good. _____

**4** **Write your own answers.**

**1** Do you know the name of the student who is sitting next to you?  If yes, what's his / her name?
_____

**2** Write two kinds of birds which cannot fly.
_____

## 1 📖 Words/Phrases

| ① | was born ( ) ___ | ⑥ | firewood ( ) ___ |
| ② | village ( ) ___ | ⑦ | float ( ) ___ |
| ③ | couple ( ) ___ | ⑧ | stream ( ) ___ |
| ④ | clothes ( ) ___ | ⑨ | mountain ( ) ___ |
| ⑤ | gather ( ) ___ | ⑩ | establish ( ) ___ |

### ○ 人をもっと詳しく説明する

The man
- who lives in that big house
- who teaches us English
- who came to meet you today
- who is dancing on the street
- you met yesterday
- I want to introduce to you

is Mr. Brown.

### ○ 物をもっと詳しく説明する

This is the map
- which shows the way to our school.
- (which) Mr. Brown bought.
- (which) Jenny drew.

This is the house
- where my grandparents used to live.
- where I was born and brought up.

The day　when we met the last time　was rainy.

## 2 Translate the phrases into Japanese. 名詞を◯で囲み、それを詳しく説明している部分に下線を引いて日本語にしましょう。

**Ex.** (the girl) who is sitting on the bench （ ベンチに座っている少女 ）

1 the city where my uncle lives （ ）

2 the bus which is bound for Shinjuku （ ）

3 the lady who is playing the piano （ ）

4 the man (whom) we met yesterday （ ）

5 the book (which) you read last week （ ）

6 the ladies who are working at the bank （ ）

7 the day when we first met （ ）

8 the man who lives next door （ ）

9 the money (which) you gave me （ ）

**3**

**3** Translate the sentences, which use the phrases from **2**, into Japanese.
**2** で書いた英語の意味に注意して次の英文を日本語にしましょう。

Do you know the girl who is sitting on the bench?

**Ex.** ( ベンチに座っている少女を知っていますか？ )

The city where my uncle lives is the capital of Australia.

**1** ( )

You have to take the bus which is bound for Shinjuku.

**2** ( )

The lady who is playing the piano is our teacher.

**3** ( )

Do you remember the name of the man (whom) we met yesterday?

**4** ( )

What is the title of the book which you read last week?

**5** ( )

The ladies who are working at the bank sometimes come here for lunch.

**6** ( )

Do you remember the day when we first met?

**7** ( )

The man who lives next door always makes noise at night.

**8** ( )

I lost the money (which) you gave me yesterday.

**9** ( )

**4** Write your own answers.

**1** I am a boy / a girl who _____

**2** I am a boy / a girl whose _____

**3** I want a _____ which _____

**4** I want to go to _____ where _____

## 1 📖 Words / Phrases　過去形と過去分詞を書きましょう。

1. finish（　　　）　finished　finished
2. go（　　　）
3. eat（　　　）
4. see（　　　）
5. do（　　　）
6. take（　　　）
7. get（　　　）
8. set（　　　）
9. clean（　　　）
10. decorate（　　　）

---

「～しちゃった（してしまった）」 現在完了（完了）

○ 「もう、～した？」「ちょうど～しちゃったところ」「まだ～してない」「もうしちゃった」と言う時は **have + 動詞の過去分詞** を使います。

□ We **have** already **read** this book.　私たちはすでにこの本を読みました。

**already** もう　　　　**just** ちょうど　　　　**yet**（疑問文で）もう…?　（否定文で）まだ…

---

## 2 Rewrite the sentences according to the example.

例にならって次の文を「ちょうど～した（しちゃった）」の形にし、それを元に疑問文、否定文を書きましょう。

**Ex.**　I saw the new bridge.　　▶ I have just seen the new bridge.
　　**Q** Have you seen the new bridge?　**not** I haven't seen the new bridge yet.

1. I read the book.　▶ _____
   **Q** _____　**not** _____

2. I cleaned my room.　▶ _____
   **Q** _____　**not** _____

3. I did my homework.　▶ _____
   **Q** _____　**not** _____

4. I had my lunch.　▶ _____
   **Q** _____　**not** _____

**3** **Complete the sentences to match the Japanese.**

**1** 私は今ちょうど札幌に着いたところです。

I _____ just _____ in Sapporo.

**2** もうあの映画を観た？

_____ you already _____ that movie?

**3** 彼女はまだ昼ご飯を食べていません。

She _____ _____ _____ lunch yet.

**4** 私は（自分の）腕時計をなくしてしまいました。

I _____ _____ my watch.

**5** もう始めましたか？

_____ you _____ yet?

**6** 今始めたところです。

I _____ just _____.

**7** 彼はもう終わっているよ。

He _____ already _____.

**8** もう魚、釣れた？

_____ you _____ any fish yet?

**4** **Complete the sentences using the phrases in the boxes below.**

**1**
A: Jenny, _____ Ken yet?

B: Yes. I _____ him.

A: When _____ him?

B: I _____ this morning.

| met him | did you meet | have you met | have already met |

**2**
A: _____ your homework yet?

B: No, I _____ it yet.

A: When _____ it?

B: I'm _____ by tomorrow afternoon.

| going to finish it | have you finished | are you going to finish | haven't finished |

## 1 📖 Words / Phrases 過去形と過去分詞を書きましょう。

① be ( ) was were    been
④ meet ( )

② draw ( )
⑤ feel ( )

③ ride ( )
⑥ make ( )

---

「今まで～したことがある（ない）」現在完了（経験）

○ 現在までの経験について話したり尋ねる時も **have + 動詞 の過去分詞** を使います。

☐ I **have seen** a ghost **before**.　私は以前、ゆうれいを見たことがあります。
☐ I **have never seen** a ghost.　私はゆうれいを見たことはありません。
☐ **Have** you **ever seen** a ghost?　今までゆうれいを見たことがありますか？

**ever** 今まで　　　　　**never** 1度も～ない　　　　　**before** 以前に

---

## 2 Translate the sentences into Japanese. 意味の違いに注意して日本語にしましょう。

① Did you go to Hokkaido? — Yes, I did. ( )

I went to Hokkaido last month. ( )

② Have they gone to Hokkaido yet? ( )

Yes, they have. ( )

They have just gone to Hokkaido. ( )

※「行ったことがある」はhave + been + to

③ Have you ever been to Hokkaido? ( )

I have been to Hokkaido before. ( )

I have never been to Hokkaido. ( )

④ Did you see a ghost? — Yes, I did. ( )

I saw a ghost yesterday. ( )

⑤ Have you ever seen a ghost before? ( )

I have seen a ghost several times. ( )

I have never seen a ghost before. ( )

**3** 「～したことがありますか」 **Rewrite the sentences into questions.**

**1** You have been to Kyoto. ▷ Have you _____

**2** Your father has been to Hawaii.
▷ _____

**3** Ben has been to Tokyo. ▷ _____

**4** Jane has seen that man before.
▷ _____

**4** 「今まで～したことがない」 **Complete the sentences using never.**

**1** I have touched a koala. ▷ _____

**2** You have been to a concert.
▷ _____

**3** Cathy has eaten space food before.
▷ _____

**5** **Write your own answers.**

**1** Have you ever been to Disneyland? _____

**2** Have you ever carved a jack-o'-lantern? _____

**3** Have you ever seen Awa Odori in Tokushima? _____

**4** Have you gone swimming recently? _____

**5** I have seen _____ before.

**6** I have never been to _____ before.

※recently - 最近

## 1 📖 Words / Phrases

**① sunset**
( ) _____

**② character**
( ) _____

**③ cartoon**
( ) _____

**④ sight**
( ) _____

**⑤ thoughtful**
( ) _____

**⑥ nicest**
( ) _____

「私が今まで〜した一番…」(最上級)

◯ **The 最上級 … (that) I have ever 〜**　　私が今まで 〜した一番…

　☐ **the biggest ice cream (that) I have ever had**　　ぼくが今まで食べた一番大きなアイスクリーム
　☐ **the most beautiful sunset (that) I have ever seen** ぼくが今まで見た一番きれいな夕日

●次のような英文でも that が使われます。

**1**　I spent all the money (that) I had.　　( )

**2**　He was the only person (that) I knew at the camp. ( )

**3**　Please tell me everything (that) you know. ( )

**4**　The first student that came to school today was Bill. ( )

## 2 Translate the sentences into Japanese. 例を参考に名詞に◯、それを修飾する語句に下線を引いて日本語にしましょう。

**Ex.** (the best movie) that I have ever seen　　　　( 私が今まで見た一番良い映画 )

**①** the longest story (that) I have ever read ( )

**②** the most expensive pen (that) I have ever bought ( )

**③** the highest mountain (that) I have ever climbed ( )

**④** The longest story (that) I've ever read is Gone with the Wind.
( )

**⑤** My mother keeps the first picture (that) I drew.
( )

**⑥** This is the biggest bird that can fly. ( )

**⑦** The best cake (that) I've ever had is the one which I bought at this shop.
( )

**3**

**3** **Complete the sentences to match the Japanese.** （　　）内の語句を補うのに適当な場所に∧を入れ、全文を書きましょう。

**1** This is the most beautiful picture. (私が今まで見た)
_____
_____

**2** He is the tallest man. (私が今まで会った)
_____
_____

**3** The most difficult language is French. (私が今まで勉強した)
_____
_____

**4** The last student is Tom. (ここに来た)
_____
_____

**5** The best essay is the one. (私が今まで読んだ) (あなたが書いた)
_____
_____

**6** The dog is the friendliest dog. （Billが飼っている）（今まで見た）
_____
_____

**4** **Complete the sentences to match the Japanese.**

**1** これは私が今まで食べた一番おいしいケーキです。
This is the most delicious cake _____

**2** 今日欠席した唯一の生徒は ケンでした。
The only student _____

**3** あなたがかばんの中に持っているものすべてを見せなさい。
Show me everything _____

**5** **Write your own answers.**

**1** What is the only animal that can fly?
_____
_____

**2** What is the best book that you've ever read?
_____
_____

**3** What is the fastest time that you've ever run the 100-meter dash?
_____
_____

**4** What is the most expensive thing that you've ever bought by yourself?
_____
_____

## 1 📖 Words/Phrases

**①** wait for
( )  _____

**②** worry about
( )  _____

**③** look for
( )  _____

**④** keep you waiting
( )  _____

**⑤** current
( )  _____

**⑥** all day
( )  _____

---

「ずっと〜（の状態）」「ずっと〜している」　現在完了（継続）と 現在完了進行形

○「ずっと〜（の状態）」「ずっと〜している」と 状態や動作が継続していることを表す時は
**have ＋ 動詞の過去分詞** または **have been ＋ …ing** を使います。

- ☑ We **have been** friends since we were kids.　　幼い時からずっと友達
- ☑ I **have wanted** to meet him for years.　　長い間 ずっと彼に会いたいと思っている
- ☑ I **have been waiting** for a phone call for three hours. 3時間ずっと電話を待っている

**since**（過去のある時点）から〜　　**for** 〜の間（期間）　　＊**be** 動詞の過去分詞は **been**

■ 状態がずっと続いている：現在完了（継続）

**1** I have been busy since this morning.　　私は朝からずっと _____ です。

**2** I have known him since I was a child.　　（ ）

**3** He has been sick in bed for two weeks.　　（ ）

■ 動作が今も続いている：現在完了進行形

**1** I have been waiting for him since this morning.　　私は朝からずっと彼を _____

**2** She has been practicing the piano for two hours.　　彼女は2時間 _____

**3** I have been studying English since I was six years old.　（ ）

**4** He has been sleeping for more than ten hours.　（ ）

---

## 2 Complete the sentences using the word since or for.

**①** He has lived in this city _____ 2000.

**②** We have been waiting for Jack _____ thirty minutes.

**③** It hasn't rained _____ two weeks.

**④** My brother has loved animals _____ he was little.

**⑤** I haven't seen my grandmother _____ a long time.

**3** **Complete the sentences to match the Japanese.**

**1** 私はこのかばんを5年使っています。

I _____ _____ _____ this bag _____ five years.

**2** 私は生まれた時からずっと東京に住んでいます。

I _____ _____ in Tokyo _____ I was born.

**3** 私は1時間以上電車を待っています。

I _____ _____ _____ for the train _____ more than one hour.

**4** 彼は何年も真理子に会っていません。

He _____ _____ seen Mariko _____ years.

**5** あなたはどのくらい日本にいるのですか？

How long _____ you _____ in Japan?

**6** 昨夜からずっと雪が降っています。

It _____ _____ snowing _____ last night.

**4** **Rewrite the sentences according to the example.** 「どのくらいの期間」を質問する文にし、答えを書きましょう。

> **Ex.** The children have been studying since this morning.
> Q: How long have the children been studying?
> A: They have been studying since this morning.

**1** Mary has been talking on the phone for more than two hours.

Q _____

A _____

**2** Tom has known that man for about five years.

Q _____

A _____

**3** Mr. and Mrs. Cate have lived in Japan since 1998.

Q _____

A _____

## 1 📖 Words/Phrases

① tiny (          ) _____

② seed (          ) _____

③ surely (          ) _____

④ happiness (          ) _____

⑤ hope (          ) _____

⑥ exchange (          ) _____

⑦ market (          ) _____

⑧ in place of (          ) _____

⑨ burst into tears (          ) _____

⑩ age (          ) _____

下線部 ___ の語に波線 〰〰 が説明を加えた文（SVOC）

☐ I make my mother happy. 　私の母を 幸せに する

| make him happy　彼を幸せに する
| call him Boss　彼をボス と呼ぶ
| name it Sakura　それを サクラと名付ける

| keep my room clean　私の部屋を きれいに 保つ
| leave me alone　私を 一人に しておく
| find it easy　それが 簡単とわかる

## 2 Translate the sentences into Japanese.

① Let's keep the door open. (                              )

② My sister named the puppy Zippy. (                              )

③ The story made me happy. (                              )

④ Please call me Mark. (                              )

## 3 Complete the sentences to match the Japanese.

① _____ your room clean. 　部屋をきれいにしておきなさい。

② We _____ that star the morning star. 　私たちはあの星を明けの明星と呼びます。

③ _____ him alone for a while. 　彼をしばらく一人にしておこう。

④ This song always _____ me happy. 　この歌はいつも私を幸せにしてくれます。

⑤ What _____ you so angry? 　何があなたをそんなに怒らせたのですか？

⑥ We should _____ it secret. 　私たちはそれを内緒にしておくべきです。

比較級 **and** 比較級 は「ますます…」を表します。

☐ **It grew taller and taller.**　それはますます高くなっていきました。

**4** **Complete the sentences using the same -er word in order to match the Japanese.**

① The days get _____ and _____ after the Spring Equinox.

春分後、日はだんだん長くなります。

② It was getting _____ and _____.

だんだん暗くなってきました。

③ The princess became _____ and _____ beautiful.

姫はますますきれいになりました。

**5** **Read the story of Jack and the Beanstalk on p.60 of the textbook and answer the questions.**

**1** What will that tiny seed give Jack?

_____

_____

**2** Where did Jack meet the old man?

_____

_____

**3** Why was Jack going to the market?

_____

_____

**4** What did Jack get in place of the cow?

_____

_____

**5** Did Jack go to the market?

_____

_____

**6** Was his mother happy to see the seed?

_____

_____

**7** What happened to the seed during the night?

_____

_____

**8** Which was higher, the top of the beanstalk or a cloud?

_____

_____

○ **過去分詞** は人や物のすぐ前かすぐ後ろに付けて「～された（されている）」ことを付け加えて、人や物をより詳しく言います。　the broken chair

○ **be動詞＋過去分詞** は「…は～されています」を表します。　The chair was broken by Tom.

○ 現在分詞と比べてみましょう。

| 現在分詞（ ～ing） | 過去分詞（PP） |
|---|---|
| 「～している（人・物）」 | 「～された（されている）人・物」 |
| **a flying bird** 飛んでいる鳥<br>**a bird flying over there** 向こうで飛んでいる鳥 | **the broken chair** 壊された椅子<br>**the chair broken by him** 彼によって壊された椅子 |
| 「…は～しています。」（be ＋ ～ing） | 「…は～されています。（されました。）」（be ＋ PP） |
| **A bird is flying.** 1羽の鳥が飛んでいます。 | **The chair was broken by Tom.** 椅子は Tom によって壊されました。<br>※（人）によっていう行為者は by を付けます。 |

**1** Complete the sentences using the correct form. 日本語に合うように speak, write の形を変えましょう。

**speak**

❶ Jack _____ English.　ジャックは英語を話します。

❷ Jack _____ English now.　ジャックは今、英語を話しています。

❸ Jack _____ English.　ジャックは英語を話しました。

❹ Jack's _____ English is very fast.　ジャックの話し言葉(=話される英語)はとても速い。

❺ The language _____ by Jack is English.　ジャックが話している言語は英語です。

❻ English _____ by many people.　英語は多くの人によって話されています。

**write**

❶ I _____ a letter once a week.　私は週に1回手紙を書きます。

❷ I _____ a letter now.　私は今手紙を書いています。

❸ I _____ a letter yesterday.　私は昨日手紙を書きました。

❹ Please send the report in _____ form.　レポートを文書(書面)で送ってください。

❺ The report _____ by Ken was great.　ケンによって書かれたレポートは素晴らしかった。

❻ This report _____ by Ken.　このレポートはケンによって書かれました。

**3**

**2** Complete the sentences using the correct form of the word in the (    ) to match the Japanese.

**1** 100人の生徒がこの会に招待されています。
One hundred students _____ to this meeting.  (invite)

**2** アンはマシューカスバートによって愛されていました。
Anne _____ by Matthew Cuthbert.  (love)

**3** この研究では50人が検査されました。
Fifty people _____ in this study.  (examine)

**4** オリンピックは1964年に東京で開催されました。
The Olympic Games _____ in Tokyo in 1964.  (hold)

**5** オリンピックは2020年に再び東京で開催されます。
The Olympic Games _____ in Tokyo again in 2020.  (hold)

**6** この席はジェームズが使っています。
This seat _____ by James.  (take)

**7** それらすべてのケーキは1時間で売り切れました。
All those cakes _____ out in one hour.  (sell)

**3** Complete the sentences choosing the correct word below and write the Japanese.

**1** The telephone was invented _____ Bell.  (                    )

**2** We were pleased _____ the results.  (                    )

**3** His name is known _____ people all over Japan.  (                    )

**4** This desk is made _____ wood.  (                    )

**5** Tofu is made _____ soybeans.  (                    )

**6** 70% of the surface of the earth is covered _____ water.  (                    )

**7** I am interested _____ space engineering.  (                    )

**8** I was surprised _____ my bad test score.  (                    )

| of | from | with | by | to | in | at |
|----|------|------|----|----|----|----|

| A — | Are you all right? | 大丈夫ですか。 |
|---|---|---|
| C — | Can I take a message? | 伝言を承りましょうか。 |
| | Can you help me with 〜? | 〜を手伝ってもらえますか。 |
| | Certainly. | かしこまりました。 |
| | Congratulations! | おめでとう! |
| G — | Good luck. | 幸運を祈っています。がんばってね。 |
| H — | Have a good time. | 楽しんできてね。 |
| | Have a nice trip. | よい旅を。 |
| | Help yourself (to 〜). | (食べ物など)をご自由にどうぞ。 |
| | Here you are. | (物を差し出して)はい、どうぞ。 |
| | Here's 〜. | 〜をどうぞ。/ ここに〜があります。 |
| | Hold on. | (電話で)切らないでお待ちください。 |
| | How about ...ing? | 〜するのはどうですか。 |
| | How long does it take to 〜? | 〜するのにどのくら時間がかかりますか。 |
| I — | I beg your pardon? | もう一度おっしゃってください。 |
| | I hear 〜. | 〜と聞いています。〜だそうですね。〜らしいです。 |
| | I hope 〜. | 〜と望んでいます。〜だといいな。 |
| | I'd be glad [happy] to. | 喜んで。 |
| | I'd love to. | ぜひそうしたいです。 |
| | I'll be right back. | すぐに戻ります。 |
| | I'll be there. | そちらへ行きます。 |
| | I'm afraid 〜. | あいにく[残念ながら] 〜です。 |
| | I'm afraid not. | 残念ながら、違います[できません]。 |
| | I'm coming. | 今行きます。 |
| | I'm just looking. | (店で)見ているだけです。 |
| | I'm not sure. | よくわかりません。 |
| | Is anything wrong? | どうかしたんですか。何か問題がありますか。 |
| | It looks like rain. | 雨が降りそうです。 |
| | It's my pleasure. | どういたしまして。 |
| J — | Just a minute [moment]. | 少々お待ちください。 |
| M — | May [Can] I help you? | いらっしゃいませ。/何か手伝いましょうか? |
| N — | Nice to see you again. | また会えてうれしいです。 |
| | No, not yet. | いいえ、まだです。 |
| | No problem. | 問題ないです。いいとも。大丈夫です。 |
| | No, thanks [thank you]. | いいえ、けっこうです。 |
| P — | Please take your time. | (急がないので)ゆっくりしてください。 |
| S — | Same to you. | あなたもね。 |
| | See you later. | また後でね。 |
| | So do [am] I. | 私も。 |
| | Sounds good [nice, great]. | 良さそうですね。 |
| T — | Take care. | (別れのあいさつとして)じゃあね。気をつけてね。 |
| | (That) sounds like fun. | 楽しそうですね。 |
| | That would be great [nice]. | それはいいですね。 |
| | That's a good idea. | それはいい考えです。 |
| | That's all. | それで全部です。 |
| | That's too bad. | それは気の毒[残念]です。 |
| | That's very kind of you. | ご親切にありがとう。 |
| W — | What do you think of 〜? | 〜をどう思いますか。 |
| | What happened? | 何があったのですか。 |
| | What's the matter with 〜? | 〜はどうしたのですか。 |
| | What's wrong with 〜? | 〜はどうしたのですか。 |
| | Why don't we 〜? | (一緒に)〜しようよ。 |
| | Why don't you 〜? | 〜しませんか? |
| | Why not? | どうして? /(提案などを受けて)もちろんです。 |

■ (   )の中に最も適当なことばを選びましょう。

❶ A: Are you going to Singapore on ( _____ ) ?
   B: No, I'm going there on vacation.

| ① job | ② business |
| ③ work | ④ office |

❷ I want to eat Japanese ( _____ ).

| ① plates | ② dishes |
| ③ forks | ④ knives |

❸ When do you ( _____ ) for Australia?

| ① go | ② come |
| ③ leave | ④ ask |

❹ If I don't call my mother when I get home,
   she ( _____ ) about me.

| ① cries | ② worries |
| ③ falls | ④ holds |

❺ It will ( _____ ) you 15 minutes to get to the museum by car.

| ① make | ② take |
| ③ go | ④ keep |

❻ Ms. Nakamoto has a little brown dog ( _____ ) Brownie.

| ① call | ② calls |
| ③ calling | ④ called |

❼ It's difficult ( _____ ) me to play the piano.

| ① of | ② for |
| ③ at | ④ in |

❽ I have two cats. One is black, ( _____ ) is white.

| ① another | ② other |
| ③ the other | ④ more |

❾ My brother didn't have ( _____ ) money to buy the watch.

| ① no | ② many |
| ③ all | ④ enough |

❿ My sister has been ( _____ ) in bed for three days.

| ① sick | ② disease |
| ③ sleep | ④ shock |

⓫ A: Did you see Judy today?
   B: No. I think she was absent ( _____ ) school today.

| ① at | ② for |
| ③ from | ④ in |

⓬ A: How ( _____ ) do you have Japanese lessons?
   B: Four times a week.

| ① many | ② much |
| ③ long | ④ often |

# Let's try. 2   for EIKEN Grade 3

■ 日本文の意味を表すように、①～⑥までをならべかえましょう。

**①** 友達と一緒に行ったコンサートはすばらしかったです。   (① my friend ② went ③ I ④ was ⑤ to ⑥ with)

The concert _____ fantastic.

**②** 明日、シンディに会うのが楽しみです。   (① to ② I'm ③ seeing ④ looking ⑤ Cindy ⑥ forward ) .

_____ tomorrow.

**③** みゆきが学校に間に合うとよいのですが。   (① Miyuki ② school ③ hope ④ gets ⑤ I ⑥ to ) .

_____ on time.

**④** ジョンがその試験に合格したと聞いてうれしいです。   (① John ② to ③ passed ④ hear ⑤ the exam ⑥ that ) .

I'm happy _____

**⑤** 慎吾からの手紙で私たちはとてもうれしくなりました。   (① happy ② us ③ Shingo ④ from ⑤ made ⑥ very ) .

The letter _____

**⑥** 私のおじはハワイに2度行ったことがあります。   (① has ② twice ③ to ④ Hawaii ⑤ been ⑥ uncle ) .

My _____

**⑦** 私は風邪をひいてキャンプに行けません。   (① go ② a cold ③ can't ④ and ⑤ have ⑥ camping ) .

I _____

**⑧** いつ、あなたにその本を返せばよいですか？   (① I ② should ③ back ④ give ⑤ to ⑥ the book ) .

When _____ you?

**⑨** 私はきのう、部屋を掃除するのにとても忙しかったです。   (① cleaning ② busy ③ was ④ I ⑤ the room ⑥ very ) .

_____ yesterday.

**⑩** 私の兄は、お金をすべて漫画本に使いました。   (① the money ② comic books ③ all ④ on ⑤ brother ⑥ spent ) .

My _____

**⑪** 私は夜中に目が覚めました。   (① the night ② of ③ up ④ woke ⑤ the middle ⑥ in ) .

I _____

**⑫** 祖母と電話で話しました。   (① grandmother ② my ③ the phone ④ to ⑤ talked ⑥ on ) .

I _____

# **L**et's try. **3** for EIKEN Grade 3

次の中から最も適切な答えを選びましょう。

❶ **Grandson**: Can I have some cookies, Grandma?

**Grandma**: Of course, Toby. ( _____ )

① That's great.
② Me, neither.
③ Good luck.
④ Help yourself.

❷ **Girl**: Have you seen my bag?

**Boy**: No, I haven't. ( _____ )

**Girl**: Yes. I can't find it anywhere.

① Can I use it?
② Do you have it?
③ Did you lose it?
④ Where is it?

❸ **Father**: You look sick. ( _____ )

**Son**: I have a bad headache.

① What's the matter?  ② Do you have it?
③ How is it going?       ④ Are you fine?

❹ **Mother**: I don't have time to take the dog for a walk.

**Daughter**: ( _____ ) I can come home early today.

① I like the dog.  ② I can't do it.
③ I'll do it.          ④ I think it's cute.

❺ **Boy**: How was the trip to London?

**Girl**: ( _____ ) I want to go there again.

① I had a problem.  ② I had a lot of fun.
③ It's next time.      ④ That's right.

❻ **Mother**: Are you ready to go to the concert?

**Daughter**: ( _____ ) I can't find my ticket.

① Let's go now.  ② Just a minute.
③ I'm ready.       ④ I'll go ahead.

❼ **Man**: Why don't we go out to dinner tonight?

**Woman**: I'd like that. ( _____ )

**Man**: Sounds great.

① Let's order some.
② What about Italian food?
③ I'll make it.
④ We have some spaghetti.

❽ **Girl**: Do you want me to help you?

**Boy**: ( _____ ) I think I can finish it on time.

① That's great. ② Yes, I do.
③ No, thanks.   ④ I hope so.

❾ **Boy**: Do you know when the town festival is?

**Girl**: ( _____ ) I'll ask my mom. She probably knows.

① I like the festival.  ② I'm not sure.
③ That's nice of you. ④ Yes, I do.

❿ **Customer**: Do you have these shoes in a different color?

**Shopkeeper**: ( _____ ) I think we have them in red.

① Let me check.
② Sorry, we don't.
③ That's a good idea.
④ I'm afraid not.

⓫ **Woman**: I'm busy this evening. How about tomorrow evening?

**Man**: ( _____ ) I'll pick you up around six o'clock. See you then.

① That'll be fine.
② Me, too.
③ It's going to be cool.
④ Sorry to hear that.

⓬ **Boy**: Tom looks happy today. ( _____ )

**Girl**: I heard he saw his favorite soccer player at the station.

① How is he?
② Do you know why?
③ I know him very well.
④ It was his pleasure.

次のE-mailのKenとPeterのやりとりについて読んで、右の質問に答えましょう。

---

From: Peter
To: Ken
Date: December 18th
Subject: Christmas Party

---

Hi, Ken! How are you? I am going to have a Christmas party this Saturday at my house at two o'clock. Are you free? Do you want to come? Of course, you can bring your little brother, too. I'm sorry, I forgot his name! The party will be fun! I had one last year, too. It snowed heavily and it was hard to get here, but everyone came and we had a great time! This morning I spoke to Jenny and Mary. They said they will come. Do you like Christmas cake? My mother will bake one. If you can come, please bring some snacks to share. I hope you can come!

Your friend,

Peter

---

From: Ken
To: Peter
Date: December 18th
Subject: Thank you!

---

Hi, Peter. A Christmas party? Great! I am free and I want to go! I'm happy it's in the afternoon because in the morning I have to sing at the nursing home Christmas concert.
I love Christmas cake! I will bring my little brother John. He loves parties! Sure, I can bring some snacks. I went to the shop yesterday, and I saw some cool Christmas balloons, too. Shall I get them to bring to the party?

Yours,

Ken

※nursing home：老人ホーム

---

From: Peter
To: Ken
Date: December 18th
Subject: I'm glad you can come!

---

Hi, Ken. I'm so glad you can come! I think I know the balloons you saw at the shop! I saw them, too. They are nice, aren't they? You don't have to get them. My mom is going to the shop today. I will ask her to buy them.

Your friend,

Peter

次の中から最も適切な答えを選び、○で囲みましょう。

**Q1 Why did Peter write to Ken?**

① Because Peter is having a Christmas party.

② Because Peter had a Christmas party last year.

③ Because Peter forgot Ken's brother's name.

④ Because Peter's mother is baking a Christmas cake.

**Q2 When did it snow heavily?**

① This morning.

② This afternoon.

③ On Saturday.

④ Last year.

**Q3 What will Ken do on Saturday afternoon?**

① Buy balloons at the shop.

② Go to the party.

③ Sing at the nursing home Christmas concert.

④ Bake a cake.

**Q4 Who will buy the balloons?**

① Ken

② Peter

③ John's mother

④ Peter's mother

次の英文を読んで、右の質問に答えましょう。

# Anna Jarvis

*The founder of Mother's Day*

Do you know when Mother's Day is? Why do we have Mother's Day? Mother's Day is a time when we can think about our mothers' hard work, love and support for us. After all, it's not easy to be a mother.

For many hundreds of years people all over the world have had many different festivals for mothers, but the current Mother's Day began in the United States a little over a hundred years ago.

Anna Jarvis was born in 1864, and is known as "the mother of Mother's Day". Anna learned a lot from her own mother who was very hard-working, very kind to all people, and very loving to Anna. Anna's mother taught Anna that mothers are more important than many people think. Anna's mother believed that a special day was needed to think about all mothers.

After Anna's mother died, Anna sent white carnation flowers to her mother's church every year. Carnations were her mother's favorite flower. White was the color of pure love. For many years Anna wrote letters to important people all over the United States, asking for a nation-wide Mother's Day. Finally, in 1914, President Woodrow Wilson declared the second Sunday of May as "Mother's Day". From the United States, Mother's Day spread to many other countries, including Japan. Some countries celebrate their own Mother's Day, not on the second Sunday of May but at different times of the year. On Mother's Day, many people give flowers, cards or gifts to their mother, or take their mother out to eat in a restaurant.

Everybody's lives are different. But everybody has a mother. So, "Mother's Day" is for everybody. This day is our day to say, "Thank you, Mom! I love you!"

※ declare：宣言する

 31

**Q1 Who is "the mother of Mother's Day?"**

① President Woodrow Wilson.

② Anna Jarvis.

③ The United States.

④ Anna Jarvis' mother.

**Q2 Anna Jarvis' mother …**

① wrote letters to important people.

② was president of the United States.

③ was hard-working, kind and loving.

④ lived in Japan.

**Q3 Why did Anna Jarvis send carnations to her mother's church?**

① Anna's mother loved the flower.

② Everybody has a mother.

③ Anna's mother loved the president.

④ There was a festival.

**Q4 What did President Woodrow Wilson declare?**

① Everybody's lives are different.

② White is the color of pure love.

③ Carnations are important.

④ Mother's Day is the second Sunday of May.

**Q5 What is this story about?**

① A letter to important people.

② A kind president.

③ A beautiful flower.

④ A special day for a family member.

No.1

① Buy a guitar.
② Give his sister his guitar.
③ Play the guitar.
④ Get his guitar from his sister.

No.2

① Next to the table.
② Against the wall.
③ In the kitchen.
④ In the party room.

No.3

① He is still at home.
② He is busy.
③ He forgot his wallet.
④ His dinner is too expensive.

No.4

① He saw a picture of it.
② To take some photos.
③ There was a festival.
④ To meet his friend.

No.5

① To ask about their homework.
② He is still at juku.
③ To go to his house.
④ She knows his cell phone number.

No.6

① She must practice hard.
② She has a lesson.
③ She didn't ask.
④ She can't skate well.

No.1

① Cathy's father.
② Bill's father.
③ Cathy's brother.
④ Bill's sister.

No.2

① Her bike has a flat tire.
② Her bike was stolen by someone.
③ Her father's bike.
④ She doesn't want to go to the park.

No.3

① Finish his homework.
② Watch a movie.
③ Go to bed.
④ Get ready for school.

No.4

① Money.
② A birthday cake.
③ A book about art.
④ A painting.

No.5

① She went to dance class.
② She went to a coffee shop.
③ She made coffee for her friend.
④ She went to her friend's house.

No.6

① Bus Number 17.
② Twenty-five minutes.
③ Thirty-five minutes.
④ Ten minutes.

## Listening Test 3

英文とそれに関する質問を聞いて、いちばん適切な答えを選びましょう。

No.1

① To Jimmy's house.
② To the hospital.
③ To the park.
④ To her grandparents' house.

No.2

① Driving for two hours.
② Meeting an astronaut.
③ Climbing a mountain.
④ Looking at the stars.

No.3

① Go to John's best friend's house.
② Have a party for John.
③ Make Chinese food.
④ Go to soccer practice.

No.4

① She went to Florida.
② She talked with her host family.
③ She bought presents for her host family.
④ She ate Japanese sweets and green tea.

No.5

① She went to school.
② She stayed home.
③ She went to the doctor.
④ She went to a party.

No.6

① E-books.
② In the garden.
③ On the sofa.
④ In her room.

## Listening Test 4

英文とそれに関する質問を聞いて、いちばん適切な答えを選びましょう。

No.1

① At 5:00.
② At his uncle's pet shop.
③ After dinner.
④ At 7:30.

No.2

① A nursing home.
② Elderly people.
③ Her sister.
④ Her after-school job.

No.3

① Climbing a mountain.
② Staying in the city.
③ Spending time at home.
④ Going hiking.

No.4

① She met a famous movie star.
② She went to Hollywood with her father.
③ He took a picture of her favorite movie star.
④ She got a T-shirt.

No.5

① Andy.
② Andy's mother.
③ Andy's sister.
④ Andy's friend.

No.6

① 100 dollars.
② 250 dollars.
③ 350 dollars.
④ She couldn't buy a new phone.

# Idioms

| | | | | |
|---|---|---|---|---|
| a few | 2, 3の | | go for a walk | 散歩に行く |
| a friend of mine | 私の友達の一人 | | go on a trip | 旅行に出かける |
| after a while | しばらくして | | go on ...ing | し続ける |
| agree with ～ | ～(人)に同意する | | graduate from ～ | ～を卒業する |
| arrive at [in] ～ | ～に到着する | | grow up | 大人になる, 成長する |
| as soon as ～ | ～するとすぐに | | have a chance to ～ | ～する機会がある |
| as usual | いつものように | | hear from ～ | ～から便りがある |
| at first | 最初は | | in front of ～ | ～の前で[に] |
| at last | ついに, とうとう | | in order to ～ | ～するために |
| at the end of ～ | ～の終わりに, ～の突き当りに | | in the middle of ～ | ～の最中に, ～の真ん中に |
| be absent from ～ | ～を休んでいる | | in time to ～ | ～するのに間に合って |
| be afraid of ～ | ～を恐れる | | leave A at home | Aを家に置き忘れる |
| be covered with ～ | ～に[で]おおわれている | | leave a message | 伝言を残す |
| be different from ～ | ～と違う | | look after | 世話する |
| be famous for ～ | ～で有名である | | look for ～ | ～を探す |
| be fond of ～ | ～が好きだ、～を好む | | look forward to ...ing | ～するのを楽しみに待つ |
| be full of ～ | ～でいっぱいである | | look like | のように見える |
| be good at ～ | ～が得意[上手]である | | make friends with ～ | ～と友達になる |
| be in a hurry | 急いて[あわてて]いる | | make up one's mind | ～しようと決心する |
| be in trouble | 困っている | | next to ～ | ～の隣に |
| be interested in ～ | ～に興味がある | | not ～ at all | まったく～ない |
| be late for ～ | ～に遅れる | | not only A but also B | AだけでなくBも |
| be made of ～ | ～(材料)でできている | | on one's [the] way home | 家に帰る途中で |
| be over | 終わる | | on one's [the] way to ～ | ～へ行く途中で |
| be poor at ～ | ～が不得意な | | one after another | 次々に |
| be proud of ～ | ～を誇りに思っている | | pick up ～ | ～を車で迎えに来る[行く], ～を拾い上げる |
| be ready for ～ | ～の準備ができている | | put on ～ | ～を着る |
| be scared of ～ | ～が怖い, ～を恐れる | | save money | 貯金する |
| be surprised at ～ | ～に驚く | | say hello to ～ | ～によろしく伝える |
| be tired of ～ | ～に飽きる[うんざりする] | | say to oneself | 思う, ひとりごとを言う |
| be worried about ～ | ～を心配している | | shake hands with ～ | ～と握手する |
| become friends with ～ | ～と友だちになる | | stand for ～ | ～を表す |
| belong to ～ | ～に所属する | | stay with ～ | ～に滞在する |
| between A and B | AとBの間に | | take ～ for a walk | ～を散歩に連れて行く |
| both A and B | AとBの両方とも | | take a rest | 休む, 休息をとる |
| come true | (夢が)実現する[かなう] | | take care of ～ | ～の世話をする |
| do one's best | 最善を尽くす | | take off | 離陸する |
| do well | うまくいく, 成功する | | take off ～ | ～を脱ぐ |
| either A or B | AかBのどちらか | | take part in ～ | ～に参加する |
| exchange A for B | AをBと交換する | | tell a lie | ウソをつく |
| fall asleep | 眠りに落ちる | | the other day | 先日 |
| first of all | まず最初に | | throw away | 捨てる |
| for a long time | 長い間 | | try on ～ | ～を試着する |
| for the first time | 初めて | | turn off ～ | (水道・ガス・明かりなど)を消す[止める] |
| from now on | これからはずっと、今後は | | turn on ～ | (水道・ガス・明かりなど)をつける[出す] |
| get off (～) | (乗り物など)(を)降りる | | turn up ～ | (テレビやラジオなど)の音量を上げる |
| get on (～) | (乗り物など)(に)乗る | | wait for ～ | ～を待つ |
| get out of ～ | ～から出る | | watch out | 用心する, 気を付ける |
| get to ～ | ～に着く | | work well | うまくいく, (薬などが)効く |
| go away | 立ち去る, (休暇などで)出かける | | write to ～ | ～に手紙を書く |

## Let's try 1 p.63

❶ ② business ❷ ② dishes ❸ ③ leave ❹ ② worries

❺ ② take ❻ ④ called ❼ ② for ❽ ③ the other

❾ ④ enough ❿ ① sick ⓫ ③ from ⓬ ④ often

## Let's try 2 p.64

❶ ③②⑤⑥①④ The concert I went to with my friend was fantastic.

❷ ②④⑥①③⑤ I'm looking forward to seeing Cindy tomorrow.

❸ ⑤③①④⑥② I hope Miyuki gets to school on time.

❹ ②④⑥①③⑤ I'm happy to hear that John passed the exam.

❺ ④③⑤②⑥① The letter from Shingo made us very happy.

❻ ⑥①⑤③④② My uncle has been to Hawaii twice.

❼ ⑤②④③①⑥ I have a cold and can't go camping.

❽ ②①④⑥③⑤ When should I give the book back to you?

❾ ④③⑥②①⑤ I was very busy cleaning the room yesterday.

❿ ⑤⑥③①④② My brother spent all the money on comic books.

⓫ ④③⑥⑤②① I woke up in the middle of the night.

⓬ ⑤④②①⑥③ I talked to my grandmother on the phone.

## Let's try 3 p.65

❶④ ❷③ ❸① ❹③ ❺② ❻② ❼② ❽③

❾② ❿① ⓫① ⓬②

## Let's try 4 p.66

Q1 ① Q2 ④ Q3 ② Q4 ④

## Let's try 5 p.68

Q1 ② Q2 ③ Q3 ① Q4 ④ Q5 ④

## Listening Test 1 p.70

**No.1** **Answer : 2**

A: Do you still have your guitar?

B: Yeah, but I hardly ever play it anymore.

A: Really?

B: Yeah… I'm going to give it to my sister.

**Question: What is the boy going to do?**

×2
(以下同じ)

**No.2** **Answer : 2**

A: Mom, where should I put these chairs for the party?

B: Hmm… put them against the wall.

A: OK. And should I put the pizza on the table?

B: No, put it in the kitchen.

**Question: Where will the boy put the chairs?**

**No. 3** **Answer : 3**

A: Sorry, but I can't go out to dinner today.

B: Why not, Terry? Are you busy?

A: No, I'm not too busy. But I left my wallet at home.

B: Don't worry about it. I'll buy you dinner. Let's go!

**Question: What is Terry's problem?**

**No.4** **Answer : 2**

A: What did you do on Sunday?

B: I went to the local shrine.

A: Why? Was there a festival?

B: No. I went to take some pictures. My friend in Canada asked me about it.

**Question: Why did the man go to the shrine?**

**No. 5** **Answer : 1**

A: Hi. This is Lucy. May I speak to Terry? I have some questions about our homework.

B: I'm sorry, but he's not here now. He's still at juku.

A: Oh, OK. I'll call him on his cell phone.

B: That's fine, but he should be home soon.

**Question: Why does Lucy want to talk with Terry?**

**No. 6** **Answer : 4**

A: Why don't you come to the ice skating rink with me tomorrow, Maggie?

B: I don't think so. I really can't skate well. But thanks for asking.

A: Really? You should come. You can practice.

B: Thanks, but not this time. I do want to take lessons someday.

**Question: Why won't Maggie go to the ice skating rink tomorrow?**

## Listening Test 2 p.70

**No. 1** **Answer : 1**

A: Hey, Bill, what does your dad do?

B: He's a lawyer. How about your dad, Cathy?

A: He's a doctor at Central Hospital.

B: Really? My sister works there as a nurse.

**Question: Who is a doctor?**

**No. 2** **Answer : 1**

A: Dad, can I borrow your bike this weekend?

B: Why? What's wrong with your bike?

A: Umm… it has a flat tire… and I want to go to the park with my friends.

B: OK, but be careful and don't forget to lock it up when you park it.

**Question: What is his daughter's problem?**

**No.3    Answer：3**

A: It's time for bed, Alex.

B: But Mom, I finished all my homework.
   And now I'm watching my favorite movie on TV.

A: You have school tomorrow, and it's already eleven thirty.

B: Oh… well… OK.

**Question: What does Alex's mother want him to do?**

**No.4    Answer：4**

A: What will you get grandpa for his birthday?

B: I don't know. I want to buy him a present, but I don't have any money.

A: Why don't you paint him a picture? You're good at art and grandpa loves your pictures.

B: That's a great idea. I'll do that.

**Question: What will the boy give his grandfather for his birthday?**

**No.5    Answer：2**

A: Have you been to the new coffee shop?

B: Yes. I went with a friend from my dance class.

A: Oh, did you go on Thursday after dance class?

B: No, I went on Friday for lunch.

**Question: What did the woman do on Friday?**

**No.6    Answer：3**

A: Excuse me. Which bus goes to the airport?

B: To the airport? Bus No. 17. It comes every 25 minutes.

A: How long does it take to get there?

B: About thirty-five minutes. The bus should be here in 10 minutes.

**Question: How long does it take to get to the airport?**

## Listening Test 3  p.71

**No. 1    Answer：1**

On Friday, Yukiko's friend Jimmy fell out of a tree in the park and broke his arm. He was in the hospital until Saturday. On Sunday, Yukiko visited him at his home.

**Question: Where did Yukiko go on Sunday?**

**No.2    Answer：4**

Yesterday evening, I took my son to the mountains to look at the stars. He had a great time. We stayed there for two hours. When we got home, he said he wants to become an astronaut.

**Question: What did the man's son enjoy doing yesterday?**

**No.3    Answer：2**

Today is John's birthday. He has soccer practice in the morning. After that, his family and friends are going to throw a surprise party for him. Everyone will wait in a Chinese restaurant, and John's best friend will take him there.

**Question: What will John's friends do today?**

**No.4    Answer：3**

Next week, Emi will go to Florida. She will stay with a host family for one week. Today, she went to the shopping mall to get presents for her host family. She bought some Japanese sweets and green tea.

**Question: What did Emi do today?**

**No.5    Answer：3**

Kelly had a headache this morning. She wanted to go to school anyway because she had a class party, but her mother made her stay home. In the afternoon, her mother took her to the doctor.

**Question: What did Kelly do in the afternoon?**

**No.6    Answer：4**

My family loves to read. I like to stretch out in my room on my bed and read e-books. So does my sister. But my parents prefer to read printed books. My mom likes to read out in the garden, and my dad usually sits on the sofa.

**Question: Where does the girl read?**

## Listening Test 4  p.71

**No.1    Answer：4**

I work at my uncle's pet shop after school. I start working at five and finish at seven-thirty. After work, I eat dinner and study.

**Question: When does the boy finish work?**

**No.2    Answer：3**

My older sister is very busy. She's a university student, but on weekends, she works as a volunteer at a nursing home. She cleans the main room, and serves meals. She says she really likes helping the elderly.

**Question: What is the girl talking about?**

**No.3    Answer：1**

Karen loves rock climbing. But she can't go often because she lives in the city. Next weekend, she's going to visit her friend's home in the mountains. She'll go rock climbing there, so she is really excited.

**Question: What is Karen looking forward to doing next weekend?**

**No.4    Answer：4**

My dad went on a business trip to Hollywood last month. I really wanted to go with him, but I couldn't. Anyway, he bought me a T-shirt there. I'm so happy. It has a picture of my favorite movie star on it.

**Question: Why is the girl happy?**

**No.5    Answer：3**

Andy usually helps his father in the garden on Sundays. But last Sunday, he had a baseball game, so he asked his sister to help. She wasn't very happy about it, but she did it.

**Question: Who helped in the garden?**

**No.6    Answer：3**

Last week, I broke my smartphone so my mom took me to buy a new one. The one I wanted cost 350 dollars, but I only had 250 dollars. I am so lucky! My mom gave me 100 dollars so I could get it. Now, I have to work hard to earn the 100 dollars.

**Question: How much was the girl's new phone?**